PLACES OF FAITH

PLACES OF FAITH

A ROAD TRIP ACROSS
AMERICA'S RELIGIOUS LANDSCAPE

Christopher P. Scheitle

& Roger Finke

OXFORD
UNIVERSITY PRESS

OXFORD
UNIVERSITY PRESS

Oxford University Press, Inc., publishes works that further
Oxford University's objective of excellence
in research, scholarship, and education.

Oxford   New York
Auckland   Cape Town   Dar es Salaam   Hong Kong   Karachi
Kuala Lumpur   Madrid   Melbourne   Mexico City   Nairobi
New Delhi   Shanghai   Taipei   Toronto

With offices in
Argentina   Austria   Brazil   Chile   Czech Republic   France   Greece
Guatemala   Hungary   Italy   Japan   Poland   Portugal   Singapore
South Korea   Switzerland   Thailand   Turkey   Ukraine   Vietnam

Published by Oxford University Press, Inc.
198 Madison Avenue, New York, New York 10016

www.oup.com

Oxford is a registered trademark of Oxford University Press

Library of Congress Cataloging-in-Publication Data
Scheitle, Christopher P., 1981–
Places of faith : a road trip across America's religious landscape /
Christopher P. Scheitle and Roger Finke.
p.   cm.
ISBN 978-0-19-979152-1 — ISBN 978-0-19-979151-4 1.
United States—Religion. I. Finke, Roger, 1954– II. Title.
BL2525.S325   2012
200.973—dc22   011010041

1 3 5 7 9 8 6 4 2

Printed in China
on acid-free paper

For our parents,

Ed and Margie Scheitle

&

Alvin and Fauneil Finke

CONTENTS

CONTENTS

PREFACE

This book is about a road trip across America. We weave through the country exploring churches in small towns and rural areas as well as the megachurches, storefronts, synagogues, Islamic centers, Eastern temples, and other places of faith in cities. Drawing on the thousands of pictures we took and the numerous conversations we held, we show you what we saw, tell you what we heard, and share our experiences.

We have each published extensively on historical and national trends in American religion, but this book is neither a history of American religion nor a statistical overview of recent trends. It is about experiencing and discovering local religious communities and traditions. We hope that our stories, pictures, and experiences will give life to otherwise lifeless statistics and bring far-removed historical accounts into closer view. We invite you to join us in discovering the religious landscape of America.

Before we begin our journey, however, we need to express our thanks to many. First, and foremost, we want to thank the hundreds of pastors, imams, bishops, priests, rabbis, and monks, along with thousands of ordinary believers, for welcoming us into their places of faith. For most congregations, we arrived unannounced. Yet, they freely shared stories and typically invited us to take pictures.

We used multiple sources for planning our trip, but some of the most useful guidance came from colleagues and friends. We are especially grateful to Kenneth Barnes, Helen Rose Ebaugh, Paul Grabill, Philip Jenkins, J. Gordon Melton, Geraldine Smith, and Catherine Wanner for their advice. After completing the trip, several gave us insightful information and comments on selected chapters, including David Briggs, Michael Emerson, Matthew Finke, Deborah Hervert, Michael Lindsay, Jennifer McClure, J. Gordon Melton, Nicole Summers, Phil Sinitiere, and David Siphron. Susan Hogan and Theo Calderara, our editors, provided helpful comments and editing throughout. In addition, we thank Theo for his support and guidance in shepherding this project to completion.

We are also grateful to our good friend and colleague Chris Bader, who was a constant source of encouragement and suggestions. A few suggestions were more amusing than helpful, but they were all welcome and fun for conversation. Finally, we offer our heartfelt thanks to Lisa and Terri for encouraging us in our adventures, even when it meant weeks away from home. They seemed amused and sometimes entertained by our travels. We're glad and grateful.

PLACES OF FAITH

INTRODUCTION

Several years ago, one of us was living in San Antonio, Texas, a city fiercely proud of its unique cultural heritage (think the Alamo). It was significant, then, when an editorial cartoon in a local paper challenged this self-image. The cartoon depicted the San Antonio skyline littered with signs for chain stores: Wal-Mart, McDonalds, Home Depot, and so forth. Below this image was a caption that sarcastically read, "Welcome to America's Most Unique City."

People likely feel that this applies to religion as well. When you go from town to town, state to state, and region to region, it is easy to think that America's religious geography is without variation. Like the chain stores in the cartoon, the ubiquitous signs of the Methodist, Baptist, Lutheran, Presbyterian, Roman Catholic, and other "typical" churches found in almost all American towns give an illusion of homogeneity. This feeling is heightened by the fact that while many people may go out of their way to try a local restaurant, few people go out of their way to explore different types of religion. So, if you attend a Baptist church (or a Lutheran, Methodist, etc.) and you see those same churches all over the nation, it is easy to conclude that things really are about the same wherever you go. But underneath this veneer of homogeneity lies a rich and varied topography of American religion.

America's religious landscape is the product of a complicated, unique, and often-misunderstood history. Despite nostalgic myths to the contrary, colonial America was not a bastion of religious freedom. Most colonies were organized around a single religion. Religious leaders had close ties to colonial leaders and little tolerance for religious outsiders. But Pennsylvania, along with Rhode Island and later New York, offered a new vision of the relationship between church and state. New freedoms were granted to virtually all religions, and no single religion was designated as the privileged establishment. With the adoption of the

A sign greeting visitors entering Huntingdon, Pennsylvania denotes some of the churches found in the town. Many of these denominations are found across the United States.

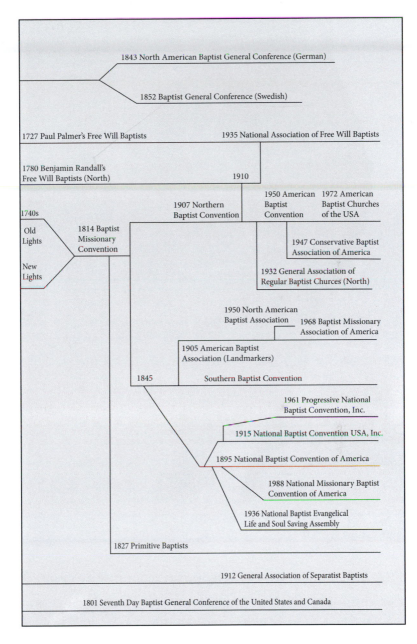

The religious freedoms found in the United States have created a dynamic environment where religious groups are formed, merged, and split over and over again. This diagram shows some of the "family tree" of Baptist denominations (Courtesy of the Association of Religion Data Archives, www.theARDA.com).

The locations we visited on our journey.

First Amendment in 1791, religious freedoms were granted, and the lively religious experiments of Pennsylvania and New York soon became the standard for the new nation.

These freedoms allowed new religious upstarts to arise and "foreign" religions to prosper. Although Methodists, Catholics, and even Mormons are now accepted as

"American" religions, in the past they were all viewed with suspicion or even disdain. In the early nineteenth century, Methodists routinely held revivals that included religious experiences considered unseemly by most and dangerous or even demonic by others. Catholics started arriving in large numbers by the middle of the nineteenth century and were often viewed as dangerous foreigners who drank too heavily and held a blind allegiance to the pope. Political movements, such as the "Know-Nothings" of the 1850s openly opposed Catholic immigration. Finally, the Mormons—members of the Church of Jesus Christ of Latter-day Saints—were considered a dangerous cult that eventually fled to the Utah desert to avoid the hostilities of the larger culture.

Today these groups are all part of the religious mainstream. Foreigners continue to arrive, and new religions still emerge. These changes are once again reshaping the religious geography of America. Like earlier trends, however, these changes are not scattered like darts thrown at a map. Social, economic, and demographic forces have carved distinctive features into the map of American religion.

THE JOURNEY

We spent five weeks in a rented Dodge Charger traveling across the country. Our intent was to follow a carefully charted 6,904-mile course, photograph key places of worship, and see the geography of American religion. See the geography of American religion we did, but we didn't exactly follow the carefully charted course. Relying on the word of locals and our good friend Google, consulting the Yellow Pages and our GPS unit, and allowing for pure chance (or providence) resulted in an endless number of welcome diversions. Who could ignore the Cowboy Church and Arena of Life rodeo center in Amarillo, Texas? How could we possibly drive by a 180-ton, 37-foot, white statue of the Virgin Mary on the otherwise empty prairie where Wyoming meets Nebraska? Everywhere we went we learned something new, like that Emmanuel Episcopal Church in western Maryland served as a stop on the Underground Railroad. We also had many curious discoveries and unexpected moments. We didn't know what to make of the ad giving away a "Catholic cat" in South Charleston, West Virginia, and we didn't know what to do when a squirrel followed us into a Roman Catholic Church in Dearborn, Michigan, and went straight to the altar. Maybe it was a "Catholic squirrel."

We invite you to join us in discovering America's rich religious mosaic by exploring some of the most distinctive and important sites within America's religious geography. Although most of our attention will focus on our nine destinations, we will offer additional "views from the road" between the chapters. Some of the views will be places we stopped along the way; others will be collections of many places. They provide still more stories from our journey. Whether the places are familiar or foreign, we are confident that, like us, you are bound to learn something new or surprising at each stop.

MEMPHIS, TENNESSEE

Memphis is one of a handful of American cities that claims the title "City of Churches." As we approached the city on Interstate 40, it seemed well-earned. Church steeples, crosses, and other religious symbols all testified to the title's accuracy. Even the least-observant driver would find it difficult to miss a few of these landmarks. There are, for example, the three giant white crosses towering from 120 to 150 feet into the air that mark the massive 400-acre campus of Bellevue Baptist Church, which lays claim to 29,000 members and boasts that two of its previous pastors served as presidents of the Southern Baptist Convention. There is also the seventy-two-foot "Statue of Liberation" at the World Overcomers Outreach Ministries Church. Holding a cross in one hand, the Ten Commandments in the other, and breaking loose from ankle shackles, this replica of the Statue of Liberty has caught the attention

The 72-foot tall Statue of Liberation marks the home of the
12,000-member World Overcomers Outreach Ministries Church. At
its unveiling in 2006, the pastor of the church declared, "This statue
proves that Jesus Christ is Lord over America, he is Lord over
Tennessee, he is Lord over Memphis."

of the national media and locals alike. The message is that
God is the source of liberation and should be the foundation of America.

Memphis's role in America's religious geography extends
far beyond these symbols, although not necessarily when
measured in height. We came to Memphis because of the
central role it has played in the history of African American Christianity and because it continues to demonstrate

the strong bond between the church and the African American community. This bond is seen throughout Memphis, both in its African American churches and in places that initially seem far removed from anything religious.

THE HISTORY

There is no denying the central role of race in the United States, from slavery to Jim Crow to contemporary discrimination and inequality. Many people, however, do not fully appreciate the way race has shaped America's religious landscape. The history of race in America produced a unique type of Christianity in the African American community that has shaped the faith and culture of blacks and whites alike.

Memphis, located on the Mississippi River, was founded in 1819 and quickly became a major port for the cotton trade. Its growth would accelerate in the 1850s as it became the hub for several railroad lines. Interestingly, the arrival of the railroad industry led to mass immigration of Irish laborers, creating a third component of racial and ethnic tension in the city, at least until the Civil War.

Black church life in antebellum Memphis was shaped by the ambivalence that Southern whites had toward African American Christianity, an ambivalence captured in an 1842 book titled *The Religious Instruction of the Negroes in the United States*. While emphasizing the duty of Christians to preach to blacks, the book also notes the need for "proper

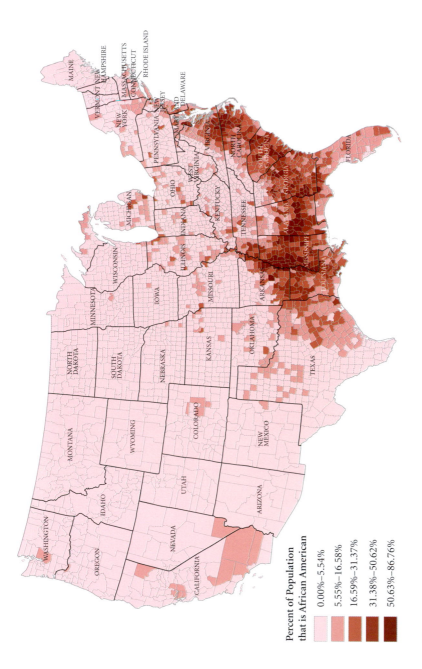

**Percent of Population
that is African American**

- 0.00%–5.54%
- 5.55%–16.58%
- 16.59%–31.37%
- 31.38%–50.62%
- 50.63%–86.76%

This map shows the percent of the population that is African American in 2006. Overall, Memphis' county is 49 percent African American. However, due to residential segregation, many of the Census tracts within the county are well over 90 percent African American.

regulation" of religious meetings and argues that independent religious organizations for blacks are "not on the whole advisable." This tension was clearly present in Memphis. Typically, blacks would attend services at white churches but had to sit in a separate area. When a handful of black congregations appeared in the 1840s, the city passed an ordinance requiring at least one white male to be in attendance, and later banned black services and ministers altogether.

Memphis seceded from the United States in 1861, but it was occupied by Union forces in 1862 and remained so until 1865. The Civil War would bring immediate and significant changes to the city, not the least of which was the growth of the black population as former slaves settled in Memphis. Long under the thumb of white congregations, the new arrivals, along with the existing black population, began to form their own independent churches. For instance, the First Baptist Church, Colored, was born from the basement of the white First Baptist Church of Memphis. Today it is known as the Beale Street Baptist Church.

In the vacuum of existing social, economic, and cultural institutions for the black population, these churches quickly became the center of the community. An analysis of accounts in the Freedman's Savings and Trust, a bank serving Memphis's black population in the postwar years, showed that 65 percent of all accounts were for churches or church-related religious societies. The position of the churches as the nexus of black organizing would have a profound influence in years to come.

Much of what occurred in Memphis in the prewar and immediate postwar years paralleled events in other Southern

Begun in 1868 and completed in 1885, Memphis' First Baptist Beale Street Church was the first brick multi-storied church built by African Americans for African Americans. It began when African American members of the white First Baptist Church started raising money for their own building. Among its many claims to the history books, it served as the site where Ida B. Wells published her anti-segregationist newspaper, *Free Speech and Headlight.* Inset: The church in the 1930s (Library of Congress, Prints and Photographs Division, Historic American Buildings Survey).

locations. Memphis, however, has played a central role in African American Christianity since that time.

THE RELIGIOUS LANDSCAPE

African American Christianity has consisted of three pre-dominant strains. The Methodist and Baptist traditions were the first two traditions to gain a foothold among the black population. The free black population in the North had created several independent denominations in these traditions long before the Southern black population was able to worship independently. The African Methodist Episcopal Church (AME) was created in 1816. Not long after, in 1821, the African Methodist Episcopal Zion Church (AME Zion) was founded. Various black Baptist associations arose around this time as well.

In the late nineteenth century, though, a form of Christianity called "holiness" began to take root among a group of African American religious leaders in the South. Originating in Methodism, the holiness movement emphasized that an individual could have a religious experience, which represented a personal connection to Jesus. This was to be attained partially through intensive religious study and practice but also through emotive experiences such as music and singing. The holiness movement evolved in the early twentieth century to emphasize the receipt of "spiritual gifts" as part of this experience. Among the more famous of these gifts was the experience of speaking in tongues. This new form of Christianity eventually became known as Pentecostalism.

Among the early black leaders in the Pentecostal movement was Charles Harrison Mason. Mason was a Memphis native who began preaching the holiness message in Arkansas and Mississippi. After participating in the famous Azusa Street Pentecostal revival in Los Angeles, Mason fully embraced Pentecostalism, including speaking in tongues. Returning to Memphis, he founded a new denomination

The sign outside the Mason Temple marks the national headquarters of the Church of God in Christ, the world's largest African American Pentecostal denomination. The Temple served as the location of the denomination's annual Holy Convocation for 102 years, until 2010, when the meeting was moved to St. Louis. The Mason Temple was also the site of Rev. Dr. Martin Luther King, Jr.'s "Mountain Top" speech, the last before his assassination.

called the Church of God in Christ (COGIC), and now Memphis serves as the administrative and spiritual center of this mostly African American denomination, which now claims more than five million adherents throughout the world.

Church of God in Christ congregations can be found throughout Memphis, but the most famous is the historic Mason Temple. Built during World War II, it was at that time the largest black-owned church building in the United States. Today, the Mason Temple serves as the world headquarters of the denomination and also as the meeting place for its annual convention, or Holy Convocation.

THE RELIGIOUS EXPERIENCE

A visitor attending services at one of Memphis's African American churches is likely to find a distinctive style of worship. Black churches tend to emphasize emotion and experience over subdued study or doctrine. Indeed, it was the lack of rigid organizational structure and staid liturgy that made the early Baptist and Methodist traditions appealing to the slave and free black populations, since they rarely had the formal education expected for participation and leadership in other traditions.

Wanting to appreciate this style in person, we sifted through the Yellow Pages, looked at online census data, and utilized our ever-helpful GPS unit to identify a small congregation just northeast of downtown Memphis. Located in a predominantly African American neighborhood was a small COGIC congregation. Given that it was near many other small congregations, it seemed like the perfect location for a Sunday visit. When we were unable to reach the church's pastor by phone, however, we decided to pay a preliminary visit on Saturday.

As we exited the freeway, the local residents immediately pegged us as strangers. Conversations seemed to end, and heads turned as we slowly drove through the neighborhood looking for churches. Of course, identifying us as outsiders wasn't particularly difficult given our touristlike picturetaking, our Pennsylvania license plates, and, perhaps most importantly, our distinct contrast from the racial composition of the area. Understandably, the neighborhood's residents were both curious about and suspicious of what was likely a rare breach of residential racial segregation.

We located the small, white, wooden First Tabernacle church. Though modest in size and appearance, it is a well-kept church that stands on a corner in a neighborhood near the freeway. After taking several pictures and having a friendly conversation with one of the neighbors, we were on our way.

The next morning we arrived at 9:40 and were warmly greeted by the congregation even though we unknowingly arrived in the midst of a Bible study. The church is led by Pastor Robert Cole Jr., who amusedly told us that a neighbor

Outside the First Tabernacle Church of God & Christ, where we attended a worship service. The congregation was at one time affiliated with the Church of God in Christ, but later became independent. However, it maintains the tradition of African American Pentecostalism.

of the church had warned him that "two white men" had been taking pictures of his church. Apparently, we were as conspicuous as we had suspected.

Pastor Cole stands well over six feet and commands a forceful voice. He converted to Christianity during an eight-year stint in prison. He described himself as a former drug addict and thief. Pastor Cole and his wife started First Tabernacle church nearly eighteen years ago in their home. A few years later they moved into their current building. When they first arrived, Cole said that "the house across the street was a drug dealer house," and the church was frequently a target of break-ins. Now, however, people in the neighborhood have gained a respect for the church and "they watch out for us." Pastor Cole told us that because of some recent changes in the Church of God in Christ, he had decided to go independent. Sure enough, when we looked more closely at the church sign we saw that it said "Church of God & Christ."

We are not sure when the Bible study began, but it continued for more than an hour after we arrived. A deacon was leading the study, and Pastor Cole sat in a chair near the pulpit, behind the deacon. When the attention of the class began to fade, Pastor Cole would arise to offer an extended commentary on the text. As the Bible class came to a close Pastor Cole called on all of the men, even the visitors, to go to a room in the back of the church for prayer. Once the prayers were completed, worship was ready to begin.

The first fifteen minutes of the service began like many Protestant services: opening prayers, songs, and Bible readings. During the next forty minutes, however, the emotionalism

Robert Cole, Jr., the pastor of the First Tabernacle Church of God & Christ. Growing up about six blocks from the church, Cole and his wife have spent most of their lives in the local Memphis neighborhood called "Little Chicago." As he put it, this is "my neighborhood," which he described as rough but getting better.

associated with the Church of God in Christ began to erupt. Hands were raised, bodies swayed, and the pastor's message evoked oral responses and cheers from the congregation. As members came forward to the altar for prayers, confessions, and blessings, Pastor Cole laid his hand on their heads and gave each member a personal blessing as well as a charge for future living. Sometimes his admonitions were personal, listing a specific trial or challenge in the person's life; other times they alluded to more general challenges faced by many. Sweating profusely and yelling into the microphone, Cole's message was delivered with a rhythm and cadence that sometimes included a rhyme. When some (including one of us) failed to come forward, he called them to the altar.

Following this highly charged time at the altar, the service seemed to wind down with testimonials, the collection of gifts, and a few songs by the choir. Then at 12:20, an hour and twenty minutes into the service, the sermon began. The deacon spoke for forty minutes and was followed by Pastor Cole, the assistant pastor, and a female leader, each of whom commented on the sermon and gave additional announcements. Following these comments the service closed with the celebration of the sacrament of Holy Communion. At 1:20 p.m., the service was over, and the fifty congregants slowly began heading for home.

When we spoke with Pastor Cole after the service, he talked openly about himself, the church, and the community. The proud father of five children, fourteen grandchildren, and one great-grandson, Cole spoke often about his concern for youth and the church's need to reach out to the community. He recounted with pride the number of young church members who had gone to college and that none of his boys had gone to jail. He also noted the strict training he gave to his young deacons. But his concerns went beyond the youth in his church. When describing kids in the neighborhood, he said that "some of them [are] bad and some of them are just running with bad people." He went on to explain that

Scenes from the worship service at the Church of God & Christ congregation.

churches should "give the young people something to look forward to, to encourage them, to tell them what they can do." Pastor Cole concluded that not only will it help the children, "it makes a better community."

BEYOND THE CHURCH

There are certain elements of a black church service that are difficult to appreciate unless you witness them in person, such as the unique cadence or rhythm of the preacher's

Mr. Handy's Blues Hall on Beale Street. A Lonely Planet travel guide describes it as "a classic juke joint, stale from the scent of 100 years of cigarettes and hard times." Beale Street, the "black main street," served as the center of African American social, economic, cultural and religious life in ways that made these elements indistinguishable from each other.

speech. One aspect of the black church service that many already appreciate, although they likely do not fully realize it, is the music. The gospel music originating from black churches has left a profound mark on Memphis, not to mention the musical culture of the United States.

Gospel music had its origins in the "spirituals" sung by slaves. Their lyrics blended slave life with Christian themes of salvation and redemption, the rhythms reflected the African heritage the slaves had brought with them to America. As it broke out of the church walls in the twentieth century, gospel music became the foundation of soul and rhythm and blues. Many of the stars of these

A blues singer performing on the Beale Street sidewalk. Blues and soul music are directly rooted in the African American church.

genres, like Aretha Franklin and Curtis Mayfield, grew up singing in church, and its influence is clear in their music. Although soul and rhythm and blues represent "popular" genres, in the early days they were not disconnected from their roots in the black church or the themes found in slave spirituals. It is no surprise that phrases such as "gospel vision" and "soul sermons" are used to describe this "popular" music.

Memphis was one of the most important centers of gospel music and the other forms that grew out of it. Beale Street, the "black Main Street," served as the center of black social, economic, and cultural life. The nightclubs on Beale Street helped develop and expand the musical forms that originated in black churches. It should be no surprise that Beale Street is also home to Tennessee's oldest surviving black church, the Beale Street Baptist Church. After a period of disuse and deterioration, Beale Street has been revived as something of a tourist destination, but it still evokes some of the spirit and meaning for locals that it once held. As if this history and tradition were not enough to attract us, we arrived during the World Championship Barbecue Cooking Contest.

Stax Records, an important producer of soul music, was also based in Memphis and is now home to the Stax Museum of American Soul Music. Often described as "gospel with secular lyrics," Ray Charles summarized soul music as the result of mixing blues, country, and the church. The museum makes the influence of the church undeniable, as display after display emphasizes the church origins of the music.

Memphis also claims the first radio station devoted to black music and entertainment, WDIA. Founded in 1948, WDIA's 50,000-watt signal reached far beyond Memphis into Mississippi, Arkansas, and Missouri. Not surprisingly, the station prominently featured gospel music and other religious programming, as well as rhythm and blues and other genres. While the mixing of religious and "secular" music offended some, the inherent connection between the two was not lost on the majority of the audience. Nor was the audience limited to blacks. The music of the black churches was soon found in some white churches and would quickly influence the secular music of whites as well, with Elvis Presley, a Memphis-area native, serving as perhaps the best-known example of a white musician drawing on the music of the black church.

The fuzzy boundary between the church and the world has long been an important characteristic of black life. We observed earlier that, in the wake of the Civil War, churches were one of the few areas where blacks could pursue social and economic activities independently. The concentration of economic, social and spiritual capital in the church meant that when it came to challenging the conditions that required that concentration in the first place—namely segregation and all it encompassed—the church played a primary role. It is not a coincidence that so many of the leaders in the Civil Rights movement had the abbreviation "Rev." in front of their names. The church was one of the few places where black leaders could be honed, so it was from the church where Civil Rights leaders were drawn. Black churches were also the organizing points for many marches, speeches, and other activities. In Memphis, the AME's Clayborn Temple was at the center of these efforts.

Many important events in the Civil Rights movement occurred in Memphis. While sit-ins were taking place all across the South in an attempt to desegregate diners and other commercial venues, Memphis was the site of several attempts to desegregate religion. One of these "kneel-ins" occurred at Overton Park, where the white Assembly of God Church (AOG) was holding a revival. A group of black students attempted to attend the revival but were arrested and

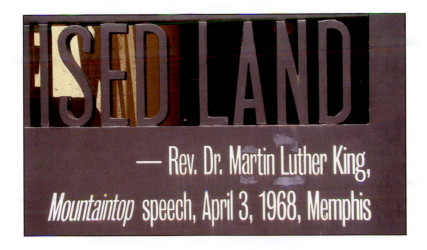

A monument outside of the National Civil Rights Museum in Memphis remembers Rev. Dr. Martin Luther King Jr.'s last speech given at the Mason Temple, the headquarters of the Church of God in Christ, the day before he was killed. The speech ended with the following: " . . . I've seen the promised land. I may not get there with you. But I want you to know tonight, that we, as a people, will get to the promised land. And I'm happy, tonight. I'm not worried about anything. I'm not fearing any man. Mine eyes have seen the glory of the coming of the Lord."

convicted of disturbing a religious ceremony. Similar kneel-ins were attempted in churches across Memphis.

Clearly the darkest moment for the Civil Rights movement was in 1968. A strike by black sanitation workers to protest unequal treatment and working conditions was building in intensity. Dr. Martin Luther King Jr. came to Memphis several times in support of the strike. On April 3, during one of his visits in support of the strike, King gave what is known as his "I've Been to the Mountaintop" speech. The speech, like several he gave in Memphis, was

The Lorraine Motel, where Rev. Dr. Martin Luther King Jr. was killed.
A wreath hangs on the balcony where he was shot. Today the motel is
the site of the National Civil Rights Museum.

held at in the Mason Temple, the COGIC headquarters.
The next day King was shot and killed at the Lorraine
Motel. A wreath hanging on the second floor of the motel,
now the home of the National Civil Rights Museum, marks
the place where Dr. King was slain.

In both good times and bad, the black church has
helped shape Memphis and, indeed, the South as a whole.

The history of the black church in Memphis demonstrates that in so many areas of life—economic, cultural, political—the church has served as the defining institution for blacks. But the city also demonstrates that its reach extends beyond the church and beyond the black population. Many people come to Memphis and go to a rhythm-and-blues club without making its connection to the gospel music of the black church. Others may read about the Civil Rights movement without fully recognizing just how central the black churches were in this history. In short, the cultural and historical geography of Memphis and similar places is in no small way its religious geography as well.

REFERENCES AND FURTHER READING

Berkeley, Kathleen C. 1991. *"Like a Plague of Locusts:" From an Antebellum Town to a New South City, Memphis Tennessee, 1850–1880.* New York: Garland Publishing, Inc.

Bond, Beverly G., and Janann Sherman. 2006. *Beale Street.* Images of America Series. Charleston, SC: Arcadia Publishing.

Curtis, Nancy C. 1996. *Black Heritage Sites: An African-American Odyssey and Finder's Guide.* Chicago: American Library Association.

Gates, Henry Louis Jr., and Cornel West. 2002. *The African-American Century: How Black Americans Have Shaped Our Country.* New York: Free Press.

Green, Laurie B. 2007. *Battling the Plantation Mentality: Memphis and the Black Freedom Struggle.* Chapel Hill: University of North Carolina Press.

Wright, Sharon D. 2000. *Race, Power and Political Emergence in Memphis.* New York: Garland Publishing.

The Underground Railroad

As we pulled off of I-68 into Cumberland, Maryland, we could see majestic old churches on the hillside overlooking the city. Each of these churches—Episcopal, Lutheran, Roman Catholic, and Presbyterian—had a rich history, but it was Emmanuel Episcopal Parish that soon captured our attention. Like the small and declining city of Cumberland, the parish has known better days. Yet, both are rich with stories that are now centuries old.

At first glance Emmanuel appears to be a stately old church with beautiful artwork. And it certainly is. It was constructed between 1848 and 1851, and modeled after a medieval English church. At the dawn of the twentieth century, the interior of the church was extensively redesigned by the highly regarded Louis Comfort Tiffany, well known for his stained-glass artwork. A local resident boasted that one of the stained-glass windows is valued at more than four million dollars. Regardless of its actual value, the beauty of the artwork is obvious to all. Yet, some of the most interesting stories about Emmanuel Parish took place under the church, where tunnels served as a final stop for the Underground Railroad. To explain the tunnels, however, we need to return to colonial days and Fort Cumberland.

When Fort Cumberland was built by the British Army in 1755, on the location where Emmanuel Parish now stands, it served to protect the westernmost edge of the British Empire in America. According to church records, George Washington surveyed the land around the

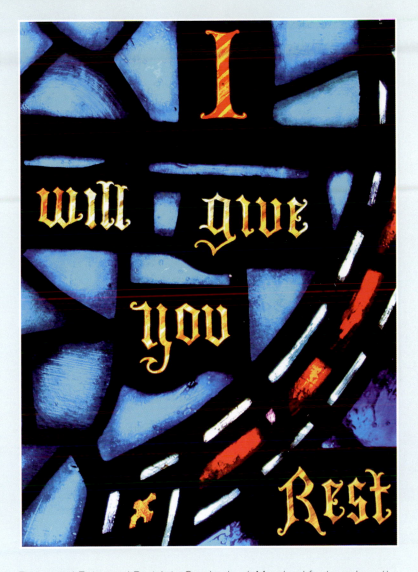

Emmanuel Episcopal Parish in Cumberland, Maryland features beautiful and complex stained glass. This portion of Emmanuel's glass might be seen as alluding to its role as a stop in the Underground Railroad, the secret chain of people and organizations that helped slaves escape the South.

Sitting on a hill, Emmanuel Parish was built on the former site of an 18th century military fort. Underneath the fort was a series of tunnels which remained after the church took over the land. These tunnels, the entrance to one of which is shown above, were important to the church's efforts to help slaves make their way to the North.

fort for the Ohio Company. All historical accounts report that it was later an outpost for then-Colonel Washington during the French and Indian War. The fort also became a location where soldiers and local residents worshiped together. When a chaplain wasn't available, the church records report that Washington, as the commander of the troops, would sometimes lead the services.

Although the wooden fort was a sizeable 400 yards by 120 yards above ground, there was also a complex system of tunnels below.

Along with serving as storage areas for gunpowder and perishable foods, the tunnels linked soldiers to the river and other areas needed for defense. The last military use of the fort was in 1794, when Washington, by then the president, returned with the army to suppress the Whiskey Rebellion. In 1800 Fort Cumberland was sold to a "combined" Episcopal and Presbyterian congregation. Overtime the combined congregation become two (Episcopal and Presbyterian), the fort was razed, and new buildings arose. But the extensive tunnels under Emmanuel Parish remained.

Just four miles south of the Mason-Dixon Line, these tunnels eventually became a final stop on the Underground Railroad. The Reverend David Hillhouse Buel, the rector of Emmanuel Parish, and Samuel Denson, an escaped slave posing as a freedman, devised a transportation system for this station of the Underground Railroad. After Buel hired Denson as the sexton (custodian) of the church, Denson's job required him to both ring the church bells and to go into the tunnels below the church. Escaped slaves were instructed to wait near the river in an area called Shanty Town and listen for a special ringing of the church bells. Once the ringing ended Denson would descend through a tunnel to the riverbank to pick them up. After receiving much-needed rest and food from Rev. Buel and other abolitionists, the escaped slaves would then take a tunnel that exited through the cellar door of the rectory (pastor's home), where transportation awaited them. Because of the secrecy required for these missions, few documents were kept. This history has relied on oral stories that have only slowly emerged. No doubt the tunnels have many stories that will remain untold.

HOUSTON, TEXAS

You have probably heard the cliché that everything is bigger in Texas. We can at least confirm that the churches seem to be doing their part to prove that true.

When asked to describe religion in Houston, one pastor told us, "the church culture is . . . on steroids." As the leader of a megachurch with multiple locations in the city, he should know. Some Houston megachurches have memberships the size of the population of a small city. Their massive facilities are rightfully labeled campuses. And their use of the most recent technology in everything from outreach to worship would make them the envy of many a large corporation.

However, as we came to discover, the story of religion in Houston is not just about size. It is about creativity and innovation. A mix of fast growth, diverse cultures, and Texan boldness has made Houston America's religious laboratory. In this chapter we explore this lab with a particular focus on some of its largest creations.

The grand opening of the Lakewood Church in Houston, Texas. The building is the former home of professional basketball's Houston Rockets. (Photo courtesy of Lakewood Church.)

THE HISTORY

Houston is currently the fourth-largest U.S. city. It was founded late—in 1837—and remained small for much of its history. Compared to other cities in the region, Houston was slow to show any signs of prominence. New Orleans, for example, was founded by the French Mississippi Company in 1718. By 1840 it was the nation's third-largest city. West of

Houston is San Antonio, which also began to form in the early 1700s. It soon became the largest Spanish settlement in Texas and the capital of the Spanish province of Tejas. But the Gulf Coast region, where Houston is situated, received little attention from the French or the Spanish.

Houston was built on land purchased by two influential entrepreneurs, the brothers Augustus and John Allen from New York, and was incorporated in June 1837. Sitting on the edge of the Buffalo Bayou, which flowed into the Galveston Bay, the new town had ready access to the Gulf of Mexico. Heavily promoted by the Allens, Houston grew throughout

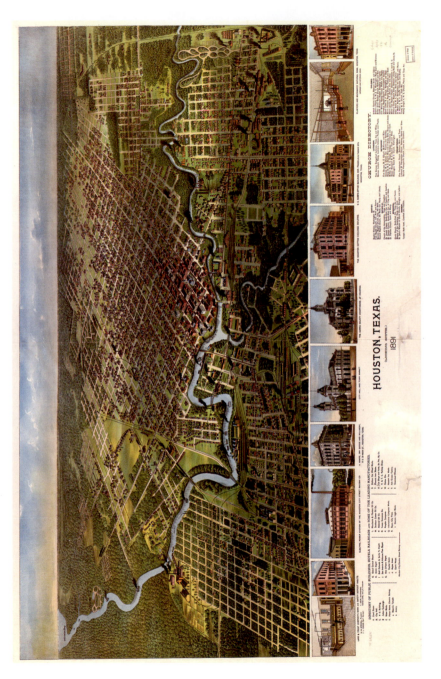

A map from 1891 shows Houston when the city was smaller than places like Wilkes-Barre, Pennsylvania and Duluth, Minnesota. The map's directory lists 39 churches. That number is over 1,600 today and includes a large number of megachurches. (Library of Congress, Geography and Map Division.)

the 1800s, but it remained a small city. By 1900 it was only the eighty-fifth largest city in the nation—still significantly smaller than cities such as Duluth, Minnesota; Des Moines, Iowa; Peoria, Illinois; and Wilkes-Barre, Pennsylvania.

At the dawn of the twentieth century two major changes transformed the young city. First, when Galveston sustained heavy damage from a hurricane, support for converting the less vulnerable Houston into a deepwater port increased. Initial funds were approved by Congress in 1902, and the Houston Ship Canal was dredged to a depth of twenty-five feet by 1914. Second, oil was discovered nearby, and the city soon became the center of the rapidly growing petroleum industry. Houston transformed quickly from a sleepy newcomer to a sprawling metro area and the largest city in the South. From 1900 to 1950 the city grew from 44,633 to 596,163. And the growth was far from over.

Despite the surge in population growth, however, Houston attracted a relatively small flow of immigrants. While 23 percent of San Antonio residents were foreign-born in 1920—a percentage often matched or exceeded by the growing urban areas to the north—Houston's home county (Harris) reported only 11 percent. The new residents of Houston were typically migrants from within the United States, with many coming from other areas of the South. As a result, by the early 1950s approximately 71 percent of religious adherents were Protestant, and most of Houston's Protestants were evangelical. The largest Protestant groups were the National Baptist Convention USA (African American), Southern Baptists, and the Methodist Church. The remaining adherents were largely Roman Catholics, with a significant number of Jews as well (3 percent).

By the close of the twentieth century, however, the demographic and religious profile of Houston had undergone a dramatic shift. In 1960 the population of Harris County was 6 percent Hispanic and less than .5 percent Asian. By 2000 it was 33 percent Hispanic and more than 6 percent Asian. The percentage of foreign-born residents jumped from less than 9 percent in 1960 to 22 percent in 2000, and was estimated at 25 percent in 2007. Even if immigration were to suddenly stop, which is unlikely, the percentage of Hispanics and Asians will continue to grow because they are much younger than the Houston population as a whole. This seismic demographic shift is resulting in equally dramatic shifts in religion.

THE RELIGIOUS LANDSCAPE

There is no shortage of large—make that very large—churches in Houston. In fact, three of the ten largest churches in the United States are located in the Houston metropolitan area. Thirty-seven churches within the Houston city limits (not including Roman Catholic congregations, which tend to be larger than Protestant congregations) report attendance of 2,000 or more each week, which is the standard definition of a megachurch. When we look at the state of Texas as a whole, there are a total of 191 megachurches.

Just as many Christian missions were quick to use the new printing technologies in the eighteenth century,

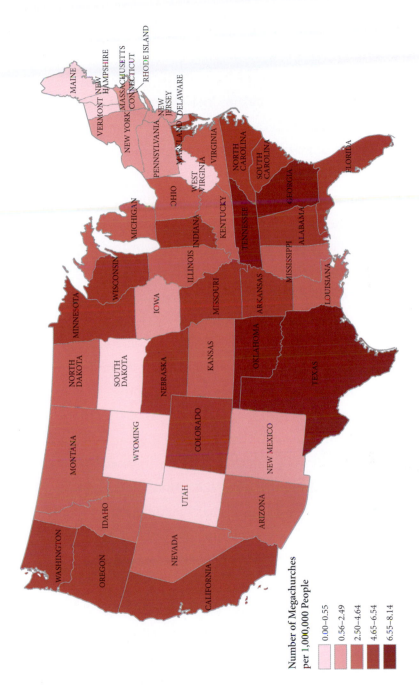

**Number of Megachurches
per 1,000,000 People**

- 0.00–0.55
- 0.56–2.49
- 2.50–4.64
- 4.65–6.54
- 6.55–8.14

Texas has an estimated 191 congregations with more than 2,000 attendees. This translates into almost eight mega-churches for every million people in the state, a rate that is near the highest in the nation. (Data courtesy of the Hartford Institute for Religion Research.)

Houston's megachurches are rapidly adapting the most effective communication technologies of today. Consider a few of the statistics reported by Lakewood Church, the home of the well-known pastor Joel Osteen. Lakewood's nationally broadcast program featuring Osteen is watched weekly on television and online by over 7 million people in nearly one hundred countries. It's also rated #1 by Nielsen Media Research in the Inspirational category. His audio podcast was one of the top five in the world, downloaded by over 52 million people annually. The websites of both Lakewood Church and Joel Osteen Ministries receive heavy traffic and offer everything from the most recent podcasts and videos to basic church schedules and service times. And Lakewood is not alone. Virtually all of the Houston megachurches we visited are taking advantage of new technologies, including social networking sites such as Facebook, to connect with their existing members and to reach out to others.

Moving beyond new technologies, Houston's megachurches are also introducing new ways of organizing. For example, a growing number now have multiple campuses. Houston's Second Baptist Church has five different worship locations with a total membership of 53,000. Like other multicampus churches in Houston, all of Second Baptist's locations have the ability to telecast messages from the main campus in Woodway or from any one of its other campuses. They vary, however, in how often they telecast sermons and other messages. Quanidos McGowen, an assistant pastor at Second Baptist's North Campus in Kingwood, explained that their campus uses telecasts only on "special" Sundays, because their campus has a sizeable staff and a large facility. The South Campus in Pearland, by contrast, rents space from a movie theater on Sunday and relies more heavily on other locations for support. As we spoke with pastors about the multicampus structure, however, it became clear that this was still an innovation in progress.

The megachurches are also adapting to the changing demographics. A growing number of the large churches now offer one or more services in Spanish as well as multiple outreach ministries to new immigrants. Lakewood Church appointed Marcos Witt as their Spanish service pastor in 2002, and by 2009 nearly 8,000 people attended the weekly Spanish service. In addition, at every worship service they have a section devoted to Spanish translation. But the targeted audiences of megachurches go well beyond ethnicity. Specific ministries and educational classes are organized according to age, gender, and marital status. Others are organized around common interests such as music, sports, and other hobbies. Still others strive to help those recovering from addictions, financial debt, or multiple other life challenges.

Perhaps the greatest organizational challenge for the megachurches, however, is finding ways of converting spectators into participants. Their size and abundant resources are assets for providing specialized ministries and enhancing the worship experience with superb music and a popular preacher. But these same assets are also liabilities. As one pastor explained: "I know people are more and more hungering for real friends. And the best way for that to happen is time and proximity." For most megachurches this means finding ways to organize members who live near each other into small groups of eight to twelve. Unlike the large, anonymous worship settings, these groups meet in members' homes on a regular basis and provide a setting where friendships can be nurtured and religious faith can be discussed and shared. Megachurches are aggressively supporting these groups by providing training for small group leaders, offering instructional materials for use in small groups, and using their websites and other Internet tools to publicize and organize the groups. Yet engaging congregants remains an ongoing challenge for the megachurches.

THE RELIGIOUS EXPERIENCE

Selecting religious services to attend in Houston wasn't easy. Like kids in a candy store we were overwhelmed with our choices. We were tempted to report on a few of the many new immigrant congregations, but we knew that ethnic congregations would be the focus of our attention in later chapters. We also thought that a sampling of home churches and strip mall churches could be interesting. In the end, however, it was hard to ignore the bright lights of Lakewood. Meeting in the former home of the National Basketball Association's Houston Rockets (the Compaq Center) since 2005, Lakewood Church is large by even Houston standards.

The church was started by John Osteen, the father of the current pastor Joel Osteen, in 1959. Initially ordained as a Southern Baptist minister in 1942, John began to stress the Pentecostal themes of spiritual power, healing, and transformation in the 1950s. Lakewood Church was an independent church that reflected his teachings. Throughout the 1980s and 1990s, his son Joel ran the media department for this growing church. A college dropout with no theological training, Joel never intended to preach. But when his father became ill in 1999, he served as a guest speaker. After his father's death, Joel continued to preach, and the church's growth skyrocketed from a membership of 8,000 to an average weekly attendance of over 40,000. The remarkable growth prompted the church to secure a $12 million thirty-year lease of the Compaq Center (they eventually bought it) and to agree to another $90 million in renovations. The new Lakewood Church has a seating capacity of 16,000 and the 2009 annual budget was $76 million.

We began our tour of Lakewood Church on a weekday, when few were present. As we entered into the building and began walking down a massive hallway we could see that the former concession areas were now converted into Resource and Information Centers. As we continued down the hallway we went past doors leading to staff offices, an expansive bookstore, educational facilities, and elevators leading to much more. We had already visited several megachurches on our tour, but Lakewood's worship area far exceeded anything we had seen. As we walked throughout the arena, some areas in the front were reserved for special ministry teams and other areas for those with special needs. An American flag hung on the back wall and a large globe was prominently displayed on the front stage. Other than the Lakewood Church logo, specific religious symbols were absent.

It was hard to escape the smiling face of Lakewood's senior pastor, Joel Osteen. A large poster of Osteen hung in the hallway, and his books, many of which feature his face on the jacket, filled the bookstore and Resource Centers. When we drove home we were greeted by a billboard bearing the same smiling face. Like his preaching, the billboard message and the titles of his books are consistently upbeat: *Become a Better You, It's Your Time, Your Best Life Now*, and *Good, Better, Blessed*. One of his favorite phrases is that "God's dream for your life is bigger than your own." We had seen Osteen's videos and were familiar with the feel-good messages from his books, but we now wanted to learn more about what isn't shown on TV or in his videos. How does a church this large operate?

Leaders of megachurches, especially those on television, often become influential far beyond the walls of their own congregation. Above is a table stacked with books, compact discs, and other items created by Lakewood Church's Joel Osteen. Osteen's materials have been wildly successful.

We arrived at the parking garage at 10:00 a.m. on Sunday, an hour before the 11:00 a.m. service. As we walked to the church we saw large signs and five-foot-high arrows directing us to the church. Along the way we even saw a storm sewer drain cover that bore the name and logo of Lakewood Church. As we walked to the church we were met by a large flow of people leaving the 8:30 a.m. service, which had just ended. When we entered the church, the bulk of the crowd was gone, but several still remained in the hallways, and many more were in the bookstore.

We began by contacting the Operations Director for Service Team Ministries, Elvin Craig. Mr. Craig explained that Lakewood couldn't hold a worship service or operate most of its ministries without volunteers. He and other staff members we spoke with noted that the number of paid employees, 350, is tiny when compared with the more than 5,000 volunteers who serve the church *each week*. For the worship service alone the number of volunteers is staggering. They have over 600 volunteer ushers, and this is only one of many volunteer groups. Even before the worship starts, volunteers direct street and pedestrian traffic, provide transportation, offer information, and give physical assistance. Once the service begins volunteers assist in child care, usher, and serve as prayer partners, choir members, and other roles in the worship service.

As we waited in the hallway before the service, we noticed that several of the early arrivals had badges that identified them as team leaders, or as being involved in a specific ministry team. When we went by the "Radio Room" we saw volunteers

As with any church, volunteers form the backbone of a megachurch.
On the left, ushers and other volunteers check-in and receive radios at
Lakewood Church. On the right, a volunteer Team Leader stands post to
assist other volunteers or attendees of the church.

going in and out to pick up radios used for communication
inside the arena. On one wall was a cabinet filled with the radios, on another a map of the different sections of the arena
where ushers were assigned. When people first began to arrive
most entrances were roped off, with only the entrances near
the front of the worship area being open. But as the seats began
to fill in the front of the arena and the flow of traffic increased,
they continued to open more entrances.

The first hour of the service was dominated by music, and
the quality of the music, as well as the quality of the sound and
video being produced, was impressive. The powerful voices of
the lead vocalists were supported by an orchestra and a choir of

A worship service at a megachurch involves a large team of technicians, both visible and behind the scenes, to operate the lights, cameras, and audio systems. The above photo shows the control booth at Lakewood Church.

over a hundred. Lights would dim slightly as meditative songs played and would brighten for upbeat praise music. Most messages and announcements were brief during this hour, but at 11:30 a.m. the audience was invited to come forward where a "prayer partner" would meet and pray with them. Then, at the end of the hour, an offering was taken. During the entire first hour the size of the audience continued to increase.

The primary focus of the service, however, was the main message or sermon that began at noon. Brian Houston, the senior pastor of a large Pentecostal megachurch in Australia, was giving the message. As Osteen does, he stressed the blessings that can be received by trusting in God's authority

With the lights, music, and impressive size of Lakewood's sanctuary creating energy and excitement, parts of the worship service can feel like a rock concert.

"Prayer partners" are stationed around Lakewood's sanctuary.

Thousands of worshipers flow out of Lakewood Church. As they exit, they walk under the church's bookstore and a quote from the Bible.

and power. He closed with a blessing, the music returned, and the crowd began to exit.

Although Sunday morning is often referred to as the most segregated time of the week, the crowd at Lakewood was a demographic reflection of the Houston area. Even when you looked within each section of the arena, most were a blend of ethnic and racial groups. Hispanics were underrepresented at the 11 a.m. service, but they would obviously be overrepresented in the Spanish service that would follow. The only imbalance appeared to be age. Despite including all age groups, the crowd appeared younger than the Houston population as a whole.

By 1 p.m. the crowd was largely gone, with only a few remaining in the bookstore and hallway. The event seemed flawless, at least to our eyes. Not only were the performances shown on TV and video a polished production, the flow of the crowd and traffic, the care of children, and the transportation for the handicapped all seemed to operate with a routine professionalism. But the day wasn't over, and they began preparing for the Spanish service.

BEYOND THE MEGACHURCH

On March 7, 2010, a headline in the *Guardian*, a major British news outlet, read "Joel Osteen: the new face of Christianity," and the first line of the article described him as the "most popular and influential pastor in the United States." Lines like this make his critics cringe. They view his "prosperity" preaching and failure to cite biblical passages as evidence that he is promoting a feel-good message with little religious content. Yet, even his critics acknowledge that Osteen and his Lakewood-based ministries are having an impact that goes far beyond Texas.

Earlier we noted that Lakewood Church's broadcast is watched weekly on television and online by more than 7 million people in nearly one hundred countries. The worship service, however, is only one of many avenues for outreach and influence. Approximately once each month Osteen and his wife, Victoria, hold events in major cities across the United States and a few other countries. During 2009 and 2010 the events—called "A Night of Hope"—typically received extensive coverage by local media and attracted thousands of participants from across the demographic spectrum. Indeed, most were held in major sports stadiums and arenas around the country, including Dodger Stadium in Los Angeles and the new Yankee Stadium in New York. Following a Night of Hope in Norfolk, a local journalist reported that "[e]ven this heathen can understand his allure. He has a plan for happiness and success."

Another avenue of influence, which has reached even more people, has been Osteen's remarkable string of best-selling books and audio books. Two of the top ten audio books (third and eighth) in 2007 were authored by Osteen. In 2008 his *Become a Better You* was number four, one notch above Barack Obama's *The Audacity of Hope*. And at the beginning of 2010 his most recent book, *It's Your Time: Activate Your Faith, Achieve Your Dreams, and Increase God's Favor*, was moving toward the top of the *New York Times* bestseller list. Regardless of the measure used, it is clear that this megachurch pastor has captured the eyes and ears of many, and is having an impact that goes far beyond his local congregation.

Of course, not all megachurch pastors have spawned their own national and international ministries. Yet, even those whose eyes are focused on the local have an impact that moves far beyond their congregation. One of the most obvious examples in Houston is the Windsor Village United Methodist Church and its senior pastor Kirbyjon Caldwell. After earning a master's degree in business administration from the Wharton School of Business, and after a brief but successful career in business, Caldwell attended seminary and became Windsor Village's pastor in 1982. At the time, the congregation had only twenty-five members. Once he launched a show on public access television, though, the numbers quickly swelled and the congregation now reports 16,000 members.

For Caldwell, however, the message was *not* just about being saved in the life hereafter or about having peace and hope for the current one. Caldwell told a *Houston Chronicle* reporter "that the Bible speaks very clearly about not only improving the lives of individuals but also improving the communities in which individuals live." As a result the church organized the "Power Connection," nine nonprofit organizations for addressing the spiritual, social, educational, and physical needs of the community. The most ambitious undertaking has been the design and building of a 234-acre village in southwest Houston. This nonprofit real estate project includes 121 new apartments for seniors, 462 new homes, a 200,000-square-foot gym and community center, services provided by the "Power Connection," as well as businesses and charter schools attracted to the area. A new sanctuary, prayer center, and more housing are to follow.

Despite Caldwell's focus on the local, he has quickly gained a national following. He has served as a spiritual advisor for both Barack Obama and George W. Bush, and he officiated at Jenna Bush's wedding. As the pastor of the largest United Methodist Church in the nation and as an African American pastor in a largely white denomination, his actions are quickly noticed. His books, such as *Entrepreneurial Faith: Launching Bold Initiatives to Expand God's Kingdom*, highlight the importance of innovation and entrepreneurship, and offer a roadmap for creating new ministries. Caldwell also holds many connections outside of "church circles," serving as a board member of Continental Airlines, the National Children's Defense Fund, and the American Cancer Society. He is a limited partner in the Miami Dolphins. Like Osteen, Caldwell is one of Houston's "celebrity" pastors.

Our focus has been on the religious innovations of megachurches, but we want to stress that religious innovations in Houston and elsewhere do not begin, or end, with megachurches. Indeed, no megachurch begins as a megachurch. As we toured the side streets and strip malls of the Houston area, we found many new churches that either flourish or flounder. These small upstarts are especially prevalent in strip malls, which have high vacancy rates and apparently lower rents. For example, on Houston's Highway 1960 we found the Northeast Houston Community Church sharing a mall with Bingo Wonderland, Cash America Pawn, Passion Cove, and Jay's Beer, Wine, and Spirits. Most of these upstarts will show little growth or will soon expire,

The next Houston megachurch might currently reside in one of the many half-vacant strip malls in the city, where start-up churches take advantage of inexpensive leases.

but a few will grow into megachurches. And even if they do not become the next Lakewood Church, Second Baptist, or Windsor Village, they are proving that religious congregations of all shapes and sizes are capable of challenging the traditional image of a church as a stand-alone building with a steeple.

Innovation, creativity, and rapid change are terms associated with high-tech businesses, not religion. The stereotype of religion is one of stability and tradition. Our experiences in Houston, however, shattered this stereotype. More so than any of the other cities we visited, Houston is a hotbed of religious innovation and change.

REFERENCES AND FURTHER READING

Buchta, Charles K. 2010. "A Night of Hope for a Heathen." *Virginian-Pilot,* August 29. Page B11.

Ebaugh, Helen Rose, and Janet Saltzman Chafetz. 2000. "Structural Adaptations in Immigrant Congregations." *Sociology of Religion* 61:135–53.

———, eds. 2000b. *Religion and the New Immigrants: Continuities and Adaptations in Immigrant Congregations.* Walnut Creek, CA: AltaMira Press.

Finke, Roger. 2004. "Innovative Returns to Tradition: Using Core Beliefs as the Foundation for Innovative Accommodation." *Journal for the Scientific Study of Religion* 43:19–34.

Hartford Institute for Religion Research: Megachurches. http://hirr.hartsem.edu/megachurch/megachurches.html, accessed May 26, 2010.

Johnson, Marguerite. 1991. *Houston: The Unknown City, 1836–1946.* College Station: Texas A&M University Press.

Kalder, Daniel. 2010. "Joel Osteen: The New Face of Christianity." *Guardian,* March 7, http://www.guardian.co.uk/world/2010/mar/07/joel-osteen-america-pastor, accessed September 7, 2010.

Klineberg, Stephen. 2008. "An Historical Overview of Immigration in Houston, Based on the Houston Area Survey." http://has.rice.edu/content.aspx?id=1748&ekmensel=c580fa7b_8_0_1748_5, accessed May 22, 2010.

Kuo, Iris. 2010. "Corinthian Village." *Houston Chronicle,* July 1, 2010. ttp://www.chron.com/disp/story.mpl/nb/bellaire/news/7090271.html, accessed September 8, 2010.

Lee, Shayne, and Phillip Luke Sinitiere. 2009. *Holy Mavericks: Evangelical Innovators and the Spiritual Marketplace.* New York: New York University Press.

McComb, David G. 1981. *Houston: A History.* Austin: University of Texas.

Thumma, Scott, and Dave Travis. 2007. *Beyond Megachurch Myths: What we can Learn from America's Largest Churches.* San Francisco, CA: Jossey-Bass.

Hispanic Influences

HOUSTON IS AN INCREDIBLY diverse place, with many cultures shaping its landscape. As you travel around the city, however, it is difficult to ignore the influence of the city's Hispanic population. While this influence is predominantly seen within typical Christian congregations, immigrants from Mexico, Central and South America, and the Caribbean have also brought with them new religious movements. They've infused indigenous beliefs and practices into the religious geography of Houston and the larger United States.

Drive down Houston's Canal Street and you will find a number of shops offering goods and services that mix beliefs and practices

In the yeberias or botanicas (herbal stores) of Houston's Canal Street a person will find a mix of Catholic folk imagery and religious goods along with herbal remedies and practices originating in Mexico, Africa, the Caribbean, and other areas.

The front of the Houston temple of the La Luz Del Mundo, a religious movement that originated in Mexico in the 1920s. It now claims over five million members and is active in dozens of nations.

originating in places such as Africa, the Caribbean, and Mexico to create a sort of folk Catholicism. The shops are filled with a mix of popular religious items, such as statues and candles, along with traditional herbal remedies. Many of these stores feature faith healers who perform traditional healing rituals.

Beyond incorporating indigenous beliefs and practices, Hispanic immigrants have also introduced entirely new religious movements. One day, as we drove down the highway, we noticed a building that looked like it had been plucked out of ancient Greece. As we would discover, this was a temple of La Luz del Mundo, or the Light of the World. La Luz del Mundo is a movement that began in Mexico. It fuses elements of Pentecostalism with unique theological and organizational features based on revelations received by its charismatic founder and the son who succeeded him.

Legend has it that Eusebio Joaquin Gonzalez began to receive revelations from God on April 6, 1926. These revelations told Gonzalez that he was to lead the restoration of the "Primitive Christian Church" and form a community of "Chosen People." He took on the name Aaron and began to preach, perform miracles, and gather his first followers, who are sometimes referred to as "Aaronites" by outsiders. Eventually, Gonzalez and his followers established a community in Guadalajara, which today has over 35,000 members and an enormous temple to which followers from around the world make pilgrimages. From this base La Luz del Mundo has vigorously pursued expansion and missionary work. While Aaron died in 1964, the work of La Luz del Mundo continues under his son, Samuel, who has accelerated the movement's growth even more. The temple in Houston is just one piece of evidence.

There is little doubt that as the Hispanic population of the United States grows, it will continue to play an increasingly important part in our religious narrative.

COLORADO SPRINGS, COLORADO

If you were dropped in an unknown place and told to map its religious geography, you would most likely begin by finding, counting, and categorizing the churches, synagogues, mosques, and other places of worship. But one lesson we have learned on our trip is that these buildings are just the beginning of religious geography.

Colorado Springs presents an interesting illustration of this point. It has been labeled the "utopia" or "Vatican" of evangelical Christianity. On the surface this would seem to be a misnomer. Neither Colorado nor Colorado Springs are even close to the top of the list of places with high rates of attendance at evangelical churches. What makes Colorado Springs a unique place in America's religious geography is its high concentration of nontraditional evangelical

Outside of a Christian parachurch organization in Colorado Springs flies the state flag of Colorado alongside a flag called the "Christian flag." Although it can be dated back to the late 19th century and is not isolated to Colorado Springs, the Christian flag is found outside many parachurch organizations within the city.

organizations. These organizations are often called "parachurch" groups or ministries. They consist mainly of nonprofits engaged in various forms of Christian outreach outside of the authority or structure of any particular church or denomination.

The parachurch sector is an influential and growing part of American religion that does not receive the attention it should. We came to Colorado Springs, the undisputed capital of the parachurch movement, to explore these organizations and their place in America's religious geography.

THE HISTORY

Most histories of Colorado begin in 1858, when rumors about the discovery of a large amount of gold in the area spread eastward. The next year more than 100,000 people flocked to Colorado with hopes of striking it rich. Most of these "fifty-niners" found the rumors of vast and easily extracted gold deposits to be greatly exaggerated and quickly returned home. Others, either because of the beauty of the landscape or because they were too poor to make the trip back, established settlements.

As was common in many Western states, the introduction of rail lines in the early 1870s dramatically accelerated Colorado's growth and development. One of these rail lines, the Denver and Rio Grande Company, passed through what is now Colorado Springs. Promoted as a resort town that would appeal to wealthy tourists looking for a safe and comfortable frontier adventure, Colorado Springs grew rapidly.

Colorado Springs remained primarily dependent on tourism for decades, but World War II soon brought military investment. After the bombing of Pearl Harbor, Camp Carson (later Fort Carson) was founded to serve as a military training facility. The creation of the North American Air Defense Command (NORAD) and the Air Force Academy in 1958 made Colorado Springs a military town.

A panoramic 1882 map of Colorado Springs. Along with ten churches, the sites marked on the map include the Garden of the Gods and Pikes Peak, which is the largest mountain in the background. Those locations are two of the city's prime tourist attractions. (Library of Congress, Geography and Map Division.)

Many people point to the relatively conservative political climate created by the city's military community as one reason why Christian parachurch organizations find the area attractive. While this may have helped its growth in later decades, the seeds of Colorado Springs' parachurch industry were planted well before the military was fully established in the city. In 1946 a Christian organization called Young Life moved to Colorado Springs from Texas. Young Life began in 1938 when Jim Rayburn, a Presbyterian minister, developed the idea of starting Christian clubs within schools to minister to youth who did not attend church. In 1941 Rayburn formally established Young Life to replicate his clubs in schools across the country. Five years later, he relocated the organization to Colorado Springs.

A few years later a real estate broker contacted Billy Graham about a vacant property in Colorado Springs called Glen Eyrie. Graham ultimately decided to pass on purchasing the property for his ministry but only after he convinced The Navigators, a Christian parachurch organization with whom Graham had previously collaborated, to purchase the property for themselves. Both Young Life and the Navigators are still headquartered in Colorado Springs.

The number of parachurch organizations in Colorado Springs accelerated rapidly in the 1980s, due to both push and pull factors. Consider the case of Focus on the Family, a well-known Christian publishing and media organization, which was originally headquartered in California. In the late 1980s, Focus on the Family began looking to move, as the cost of doing business in California was becoming too high.

Young Life is one of the oldest Christian parachurch organizations in Colorado Springs. Above is a statue located outside its headquarters. The organization offers clubs, mission trips, camps and other activities for young children, teenagers, and young adults.

But it was not just happenstance that led the organization to Colorado Springs. There was an active effort on the part of city officials to recruit Christian organizations. Leaders of the Colorado Springs' Economic Development Corporation, in particular a woman named Alice Worrell, reached out to Christian organizations to convince them to relocate to the city. Worrell benefited from her contacts and experiences growing up as the child of parents who taught at an evangelical college. As Worrell told a local newspaper, "being a Christian, it gives me a special pleasure and rewarding feeling to be able to work with these kinds of people." Her personal touch worked, as she convinced Focus on the Family and dozens of other organizations to settle in Colorado Springs.

Just as Detroit and Pittsburgh were built around the automobile and steel industries, each ministry that settled in Colorado Springs added to the city's reputation as a nexus of parachurch activity. Time and time again we were told that many of the initial moves were prompted by the lure of lower land values and a location where nonprofit organizations could grow. More recently, however, the existing parachurch network has become one of the primary draws.

While this helps explain why Colorado Springs became a destination for these parachurch organizations, the growth of the parachurch industry itself has a history. Religious ventures independent from churches were not unknown before the late twentieth century. Bible, missionary, Sunday School, and moral societies date back to the seventeenth century and flourished in the United States in the nineteenth century. Many of these religious outreach activities, however, were taken over by denominational organizations. In the last fifty years, though, the growth of nondenominational churches and the decline of denominationally sponsored outreach have created opportunities for a new age of parachurch organizations to grow. Many have chosen to grow in Colorado Springs.

Christian Organizations in Colorado Springs and Vicinity

WorkPlace Influence
on Training Int'l
Greater Europe Mission
VisionQuest Alliance
On Target Ministries
World Orphans

MONUMENT 105

BLACK FOREST

Generations of Virtue

ome Ministries

Barnabas International
Bethesda Associates
Mission of Mercy
Global Mapping International

83

Harvestime International Network

Dave Dravecky Outreach of Hope
Officers Christian Fellowship

25

Gospel of Glory
Nicky Cruz Outreach
Compassion International

Air Force
Academy

Interquest

International Bible Society
World Prayer Center

83

Christian Booksellers Assoc
Children's HopeChest

Focus on the Family and
Focus on the Family Inst

Briargate Pkwy

Austin Bluffs

Christian and Missionary Alliance
Assoc. of Christian Schools Int'l

Every Home for Christ
Joshua Project II
World by Radio
Leadership Transformations, Inc.

Research

KTLF/KTPL

Lydia Press Ministries

Woodmen

Colorado Christian University
Int'l Christian Technologists Assoc
International Students, Inc.

Global Action

David C. Cook/Cook International

Woodman

All About GOD Ministries

Barnabas Int'l
Hoops of Hope

Sure Passage

KBIQ, KGFT

Cornerstone Credit Counselors

Centennial

Christian Camp and Conf. Assoc.
Life Training Inst

Assemblies of God (Rocky Mn Dist)
Genesis Search

New Hope Int'l

OC International
CCC, Jesus Film, Here's Life Intercity, Life Builders,
International School Project, Athletes in Action
Global Harvest Ministries

Networking in Christ
Pikes Peak Academy
Andrew Wommack Min

Develop. Assoc. Int'l
Envoy Financial

Academy

Austin Bluffs

Worldwide Discipleship

International Network

Christian Friends of Israeli Comm

Garden of the Gods

YWAM Strategic Frontiers

The Word for the Word

Operation Reveille

NavPress
Navigators
World, Impact for Life

HCJB Global

WorldChristian.com, Int'l Comm Network

Entrust

ership Alliance, Waterstone

VisionTrust International

Palmer
Park

Powers

24

Fillmore

PPNC Bible College
S. Colorado Youth for Christ

Young Life Service Center
Military Comm. Youth Ministries

New Geneva Theological Seminary
Salvation Army

Colo Springs Pregnancy Center

24

91

John Jay Institute for Truth

Platte

KCBR, KCMN

Engineering Ministries Int'l

Fuller Theological Seminary

Music Evangelism Foundation

Fellowship of Christian Cowboys

Springs Rescue Mission

Nazarene Bible College

Colorado
Springs
Airport

Family Life Services

24

Fountain

Lake

Each red triangle on this map represents the location of a Christian parachurch organization in Colorado Springs. Although over seventy organizations are marked on the map, there are many others not shown. (Map courtesy of Global Mapping International and International Bible Society.)

THE RELIGIOUS LANDSCAPE

While the number is always fluctuating, there are at least one hundred parachurch Christian ministries in and around Colorado Springs. It is difficult to drive down a street without seeing a sign marking the offices of some parachurch organization—at least four were within a few blocks of our hotel. (While we would like to claim otherwise, this was not the result of our expert location scouting.) When searching for parachurch organizations, you must adjust your expectations about what a "religious organization" looks like. Most parachurch ministries are located in ordinary office buildings, often alongside secular businesses. Inside you will find cubicles and CEOs instead of pews and pastors.

Focus on the Family is still one of the anchors of Colorado Springs' parachurch community. It draws enough visitors to warrant its own signs on the freeway to direct drivers

Focus on the Family is one of the more well-known parachurch organizations to call Colorado Springs home. Its multi-building campus attracts enough visitors to warrant an exit sign on the freeway.

to its headquarters. Its high profile is not always admired by leaders of other Christian organizations in the city. This is partly because of the politicized nature of many of Focus on the Family's activities but also because the attention it garners overshadows the wide variety of ministries in Colorado Springs. Indeed, nearly every activity in which parachurch organizations are involved is represented in Colorado Springs.

Relief and development organizations tend to be among the best-known and largest parachurch agencies. They include such names as Habitat for Humanity and Feed the Children. It also includes Compassion International, one of the largest Christian organizations in Colorado Springs. With more than $300 million in annual revenue, Compassion's primary mission is to support child development around the world, which it does by asking donors to "sponsor" a child. These funds are then used for health, education, and other programs. Compassion was created in the 1950s by the Reverend Everett Swenson after he saw the needs of orphaned children during the Korean War. The effort was given its name in 1963 and moved to Colorado Springs in 1980.

Missionary work and organizations also have a long history in the parachurch sector. Many people might think of missionary work as a sole person being sent off into the world with a Bible and the intent to convert others. While there are still people taking this path, the technology and the goals of missionary work have evolved greatly. Not surprisingly, Colorado Springs is home to some of the more innovative and sophisticated examples of missionary work. This includes everything from the latest technologies in building and communications to sophisticated databases and mapping.

Among the oldest parachurch agencies are those translating and distributing Bibles and other religious literature. Indeed, Bible and tract "societies" date back to the late eighteenth century. By the early nineteenth century, almost every town had at least one tract or Bible society raising money to support publishing efforts. Eventually, the economics of publishing and increased competition from denominational agencies led to the consolidation of these local societies into a few larger parachurch agencies, most of which still operate today.

The International Bible Society reflects this history. Founded in 1809 in New York City as the New York Bible Society, it supported foreign missionaries, distributed Bibles to sailors, prisoners, soldiers, and immigrants, translated the

One of the largest parachurch organizations in Colorado Springs is Compassion International. The organization provides humanitarian assistance for children in other nations. To the right is a Compassion sticker on a car in a Colorado Springs parking lot.

Bible into hundreds of languages, and created the New International Version (NIV) of the Bible, which remains one of the most widely read translations. In 1989 the Society moved from its East Coast home to Colorado Springs. Today, the organization employs more than one hundred people at its headquarters.

Like any place with a highly concentrated industry, Colorado Springs has sub-industries that help support parachurch organizations. One example is the Evangelical Christian Credit Union. Although it is primarily headquartered in California, it is no coincidence that the financial institution's only other office is in Colorado Springs. In addition to serving individuals, schools, and churches, the credit union provides funding and other support for many of the parachurch organizations in Colorado Springs and elsewhere. There is also a variety of professional associations for parachurch organizations and their leaders, which provide opportunities to network. One such organization is the Christian Booksellers Association, which represents a wide range of individuals and retailers in addition to booksellers. Like any other professional association, the organization holds conferences, distributes a magazine, and provides support services for its members.

The density of parachurch organizations in the area can have its drawbacks. The president of one agency observed that local fund-raising can be difficult, especially for any parachurch group that does not have a national reach. It is like a neighborhood where every house contains a cookie-selling

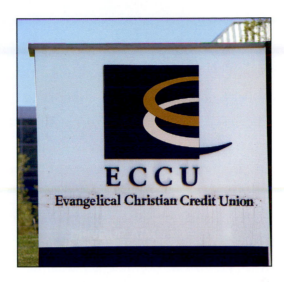

The Evangelical Christian Credit Union is just one example of the structures that exist in Colorado Springs to support its parachurch industry.

Organizations devoted to translating, publishing and distributing the Bible are among the oldest parachurch organizations. Above are some historic editions of the Bible displayed in the museum of the International Bible Society in Colorado Springs.

Girl Scout. You'd better be the first to knock on doors or have something unique to offer because the odds are that the people in the neighborhood have already bought the cookies.

On the other hand, many people we spoke to noted that Colorado Springs offers the ability to network and cooperate with others working in parachurch organizations that is not found anywhere else. There is a local chapter of the Christian Leadership Alliance, a professional association described as the "most dynamic" chapter in the country. Many of the larger parachurch organizations in Colorado Springs participate in the Community Roundtable, which helps to provide support to local social service organizations. The Roundtable allows the parachurch community to give back to the city that has obviously provided a good home for their organizations.

THE RELIGIOUS EXPERIENCE

It is difficult to describe the religious experience offered by a parachurch organization. While Colorado Springs serves as the home for many of the organizations' headquarters and warehouses, their actual activities take place around the country and the world. More importantly, there are many different types of organizations all offering a variety of services, activities, and resources. There is no single parachurch experience, we were quick to discover.

One of our most enjoyable visits almost did not happen. We were receiving a tour of an organization called Bibles for the World, which distributes Bibles and other literature, mainly in India. As our tour was coming to a close, the director asked whether we had visited the group "down the hall." To which we replied, "what group down the hall?"

She went on to explain that at one time Bibles for the World distributed their books through the mail, utilizing a warehouse attached to their offices. When they decided to print and distribute the Bibles in India, they were left with a large empty building. In Colorado Springs, though, there is always another start-up or expanding ministry looking for space. Mel Goebel had been operating Impact for Life, an organization that serves prisoners and their families, out of his home. Hearing about the vacant warehouse through parachurch social networks in Colorado Springs, Goebel moved his growing ministry into the building.

We walked down the hall and introduced ourselves to Mel, thinking that he would not have the time to speak with two strangers who did not have an appointment. On the contrary, Mel was thrilled to share the story of Impact for Life. In fact, we could barely keep up with him as he showed us around his office and warehouse. Mel's energy reminded us that, while parachurch leaders may not be traditional religious leaders like priests or ministers, they clearly hold the same passion and inspiration for doing work in the name of their faith.

As Mel explained, Impact for Life actually consists of three interrelated activities. The first, Library of Hope, provides Bibles, Christian-themed books, CDs, and other resources for prison chaplains and libraries. These materials are donated to Impact for Life by publishers and other parachurch organizations. The second program is called Kids

Mel Goebel, the founder of Impact for Life Ministries, stands in front of "Library of Hope" boxes ready to be shipped to prisons. In the warehouse, a variety of Christian books, CDs, and other materials are packed underneath a banner that says, "Let the World Read God's Word." The mission of the organization was inspired by Goebel's own experience as a former prisoner who credits Christianity with helping him get his life back on track.

Crossing and provides Christian materials for the children of prisoners. The third program, Daughters of Destiny, provides Christian outreach and mentoring for women who are in prison and those recently released. The goal of all of this is not simply to convince prisoners to become Christians (or to become better Christians) but to help prevent them from returning to prison.

Impact for Life is inspired by Mel's own experiences. He spent five years in the Nebraska State Penitentiary after a series of arrests for possession of drugs and theft. While in prison, Mel became a devoted Christian and started to study the Bible with other inmates. "With the friendship of other Christian men also behind bars, encouragement from the Bible, and the support from men who came to visit us in prison, my life slowly began to change." After getting out of prison, Mel got involved in a national organization called Prison Fellowship and later served as its Nebraska coordinator. He traveled across the state speaking in churches and prisons. In 1986 the Nebraska governor pardoned Mel for his previous offences. Mel would go on to recount his story in a memoir, *The Unseen Presence: One Man's Journey to Freedom*, which is included in many of the packages that Impact for Life ministries distributes to prisons.

The story of Impact for Life illustrates how the religious geography of Colorado Springs makes a difference. It helped Mel find a space for his new ministry and secure the donations to launch his first program, Library of Hope. Relying on more than thirty publishers and media producers to donate Bibles, devotionals, and other materials to prison libraries, Colorado Springs gave him personal contacts with many of the organizations that supported his mission and had the resources to make these donations. But the story of Mel's ministry and the many other parachurch groups doesn't stop in Colorado Springs.

BEYOND THE PARACHURCH BUILDING

Along with reshaping the local religious geography, the one hundred-plus parachurch organizations of Colorado Springs are also having a global impact. Karen Rayer, the director of communications at the International Bible Society, said that she can seldom take a flight without hearing "people in the airport and people around [her] talking about their mission trip" or some other activity related to one of the local parachurch organizations. The global reach of her own organization offers one example. Because they work with more than three hundred translators—most of them working in their home nations—the International Bible Society has networks that span the globe. The networks are even more extensive, and more rapidly growing, for Compassion International. When that organization moved to Colorado Springs in 2001, it assisted 500,000 children in twenty countries. By 2008 Compassion was operating in more than twenty-four nations and assisting more than one million children.

The global outreach of the largest parachurch organizations, however, is often assisted by a host of smaller, more specialized parachurch groups. For example, Engineering Ministries International enlists the volunteer efforts of engineers, architects, construction workers, and other skilled workers to help build much-needed infrastructure around the world. This includes schools, roads, drinking water projects, and churches. Because of its skilled staff and resources, Engineering Ministries assists many other parachurch organizations with technical expertise in construction projects. And, though relatively small when compared to the parachurch organizations just reviewed, Engineering Ministries has worked in eighty countries since its founding in 1982. During 2009 alone, it worked on seventy-four construction projects and donated more than 56,392 hours of service.

Yet another example of sophisticated, highly skilled missionary work is Global Mapping International. They specialize in providing data and research for other missionary organizations to better understand the place and people they are serving, regardless of what their ultimate aims may be. As their name makes clear, one of Global Mapping International's

On the left, the President of Global Mapping International, Mike O'Rear, looks over a world map of religion produced by his organization. On the right, an employee of Global Mapping works on a map of India.

primary activities is to provide sophisticated mapping of an area's social and religious geography. Mike O'Rear, the president of Global Mapping, reported that thanks to Skype, "on an average day members of our staff are spending two or three hours a day in conversations with people in India, South Africa, China" and other countries across the globe.

Not all of the organizations target other countries for their missions. A few are more local in their focus, and many are national. One of the most visible examples is Focus on the Family. Using publications, radio programs, podcasts, training seminars, and a long list of other programs and media, its outreach extends across the nation. Once again, the International Bible Society serves as an example. It has produced a wide range of specialized Bibles and Bible resources for populations such as cowboys, athletes, truck drivers, and for each branch of the U.S. military. The International Bible Society has also teamed with the Fellowship of Christian Athletes, Campus Crusade for Christ, Prison Ministries, Prison Fellowship, and other pararchurch organizations to increase the presence of their publications throughout America.

There are many numerical indicators that point to the extensive impact of parachurch groups in Colorado Springs, but perhaps the most convincing evidence comes from what we saw in the local churches. From the missions supported by local churches to the publications used, parachurch activities and products were seemingly ubiquitous in many of the churches we visited. Independent churches were the heaviest users of these services, but most churches had ties to these groups without even knowing it. Whether it was sponsoring children in Zambia or providing materials for a Sunday school in Atlanta, the outreach of these parachurch organizations goes far beyond Colorado Springs.

REFERENCES AND FURTHER READING

Abbott, Carl, Stephen J. Leonard, and David McComb. 1994. *Colorado: A History of the Centennial State.* Niwot, CO: University Press of Colorado.

Athearn, Robert G. 1976. *The Coloradans.* Albuquerque: University of New Mexico Press.

Berwanger, Eugene H. 2007. *The Rise of the Centennial State: Colorado Territory*, 1861–1876. Urbana: University of Illinois Press.

Ellis, Richard N., and Duane A. Smith. 2005. *Colorado: A History in Photographs.* Boulder: University Press of Colorado.

Finley, Bruce. October 28, 1996. "Springs Owes Revival in Part to Ministries: Development Official Planted Seed." *Denver Post.* Denver, CO.

Goebel, Mel. 2001. *The Unseen Presence: One Man's Journey to Freedom.* Kalispell, MT: Prison Impact Ministries.

Hazlehurst, John. January 26, 2007. "Colorado Springs: Growth Takes Root in Boom-Bust Cycles." *Colorado Springs Business Journal.* Colorado Springs, CO.

Rabey, Steve. November 24, 1991. "Evangelical Groups Reach Out to World from Springs Home: City Gaining Reputation as a Center of Religion." *Gazette.* Colorado Springs, CO.

Scheitle, Christopher P. 2010. *Beyond the Congregation: The World of Christian Nonprofits.* New York: Oxford University Press.

Cowboy Church

LOCATED ON THE SOUTHERN EDGE of Amarillo, the Cowboy Church was easy to find. We approached a large building with "Cowboy Church" prominently displayed on the front. Right on cue, a tumbleweed blew through the parking lot.

When entering the parking lot for Amarillo's Cowboy Church you drive through a ranch-style gate with the name of the church and three crosses on top. In front of the church is a statue of a horse with pictures painted on its side, and to the right of the church is a construction trailer with the church's logo on it. Two pickup trucks were parked out front, and as we approached the front door we saw a horseshoe hanging on the wall with the word "welcome" cut into it.

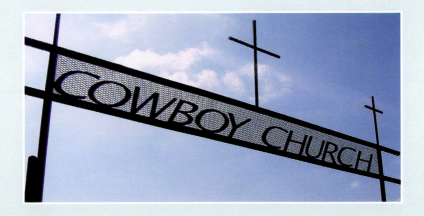

The entrance to Amarillo's Cowboy Church has the feel of a ranch gate.

Once you enter the church building, cowboy designs and decorations are everywhere. There is a wagonwheel chandelier decorated with horseshoes and metal horses appearing to run around the top of the wheel. On the floor is a small rug with the Cowboy Church's logo, and to the side is a wooden sign hanging from a post with the words "Ranchers of the Kingdom" and a cross burned into the wood. Inside the gift shop, you'll find music, jewelry, crosses, and clothing that all bear country and cowboy themes. The cowboy theme is less prominent in the "GRIT" building, which houses the church's youth ministry. Here, horseshoes and lassos give way to video games, a pool table, air hockey, and a fully furnished kitchen, but touches of the cowboy theme remain.

The real jewel of the Cowboy Church, however, is actually located out back, where a building called the "Arena of Life" houses an indoor rodeo facility. The arena is surrounded by corrals and cattle panels for taking livestock in and out of the building. Inside is a large open area where the church holds weekly rodeo events like "Team Roping and Bible Study" and "Bibles and Barrels."

Believe it or not, this is just one example of a growing number of such cowboy-themed churches, most of which are located in Texas and Oklahoma. When we asked the assistant pastor about the growing number of "cowboy churches," he explained that in many of these churches the pastor just wears some cowboy attire, uses some cowboy gospel music, and calls it a cowboy church. But, he quickly added: "*we're* the real thing." By hosting rodeo events in its arena, they have attracted a membership of "real" cowboys and cowgirls. Several of the members, including the head pastor Ty Jones, once rode in the professional rodeo circuit. Now, a few years past his rodeo-riding prime, Pastor Jones remains a full-time cattle buyer as well as a pastor.

The cowboy theme extends right down to the light sconces. The church's rodeo arena sits behind the sanctuary.

Their appeal to those in the area seems to be working. The founding pastors, Ty and Lou Ann Jones, started the church in 1997 with around forty-five members. Today the church holds two Sunday worship services that attract an estimated five hundred people. When asked if they hold an affiliation with a larger denomination, we were told that the standard answer is that they belong to the B-I-B-L-E. One of their brochures states that their vision is to share the "Gospel in a simple-to-understand practical style each week." From what we saw and heard, everything about this congregation is no nonsense, straight forward, and *cowboy*.

FOUR

SAN FRANCISCO, CALIFORNIA

Many would argue that California has played a unique role in weaving the cultural fabric of the United States. As the home of the film and television industry, California has both reflected and shaped our society's imagination. It has long been the destination of choice for treasure seekers, whether that treasure be gold, fame, or just a fresh start.

California has also been home to significant religious experimentation. The Los Angeles journalist Farnsworth Crowder once said that "the South of California has gathered the largest and most miscellaneous assortment of Messiahs, Sorcerers, Saints and Seers known to the history of aberrations." California has also played a central role in introducing Asian religions to the United States, particularly those from China and Japan. For example, a recent national survey found 648 Buddhist centers in California, which is well over four times the number found in any other state. The diffusion

Looking out on the streets of San Francisco's Chinatown from a third-floor Taoist temple.

of Buddhism, Taoism, and other faiths are reflected in both formal adherence to these traditions by immigrants and converts as well as in popular interest in concepts such as Zen. As we will see, California's spiritual creativity and Asian influences are still quite strong.

THE HISTORY

The city we know today as San Francisco began as a Mexican village called Yerba Buena. When the United States acquired California in 1848, at the conclusion of the Mexican-American War, the town consisted of about nine hundred people. Two hundred of these individuals were recent Mormon immigrants who had fled persecution in the East. San Francisco's size and history would change dramatically with the discovery of gold in 1849, which drew hundreds of thousands of wealth-seekers to California. By 1850 the city's population was over 25,000, and by 1860 it was 55,000.

But it wasn't just rapid growth that defined the new San Francisco; it was the diversity of the population. From 1870 to 1890 the city was one of the most diverse in the nation, with a higher percentage of foreign-born residents—mainly Irish, Germans, Italians—than cities such as New York and Boston.

At the time, men dominated San Francisco's population. Following the peak of the gold rush, California was 92 percent male. Ten years later, San Francisco remained over 61 percent male. Men of the nineteenth century (like men of any century) tended to be less religious and engage in more criminal and deviant behavior than women. Plus, when you have a

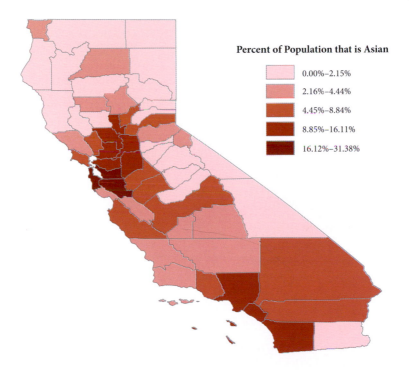

Percent of Population that is Asian

- 0.00%–2.15%
- 2.16%–4.44%
- 4.45%–8.84%
- 8.85%–16.11%
- 16.12%–31.38%

This map shows the estimated Asian population in 2007. California (in particular the San Francisco-San Jose area) has one of the highest concentrations of Asians in the United States. (Data Source: United States Census Bureau.)

higher percentage of men, they tend to be even less religious and engage in even more criminal acts. As a result, San Francisco began as a diverse frontier town with an abundance of crime and a shortage of organized religion. When one priest wrote home to his Irish seminary in 1853, he complained about how the residents' "rage for dueling, the passion for gambling and [their] barefaced depravity prevail to a frightful degree."

Most of San Francisco's immigrant groups originated from across the Atlantic, and many would gradually affiliate with the Roman Catholic Church. But some crossed another ocean on their way to California and brought religions that seemed even more foreign to Americans than Catholicism. Coming mainly from the Canton Province and attracted by rumors of *gum sham*, or a "mountain of gold," the first Chinese immigrants arrived in San Francisco in 1850. While they came for gold, these Chinese immigrants played an important role in the railroad industry. Construction on the western part of the transcontinental railroad was suffering from a shortage of laborers willing to do the difficult work. As a result, railroad managers began to recruit Chinese workers. By 1868 more than 12,000 Chinese men were working on the railroad, making up over 80 percent of its entire workforce.

Despite their contribution, the Chinese population in San Francisco and in California as a whole faced a great deal of hostility. The governor of California vowed in 1862 to prevent the "dregs of Asia" from ruining the state. This prejudice was partly a function of economic competition, but it was also a product of other immigrant groups using the Chinese as a way to establish their own credentials as white Americans.

A mural on the exterior wall of a building in San Francisco's Chinatown commemorates the role of Chinese immigrants in the construction of the Transcontinental Railroad. On April 28, 1868 workers laid down 10 miles of track, a record at the time for the most in a single day.

Hostilities culminated in the 1882 Chinese Exclusion Act, which stopped all Chinese immigration and prevented those already within the United States from becoming citizens.

An unintended consequence was an increase in Japanese immigration, as employers looked to find a new source of labor. This, however, produced similar tensions, or what many in California referred to as "the Japanese problem"—a "problem" that included a new religion. The Buddhist Church of San Francisco was founded in 1898, and a year later two Buddhist missionaries arrived. The *San Francisco Chronicle* took pictures of the missionaries in their robes and warned readers that "[t]hey will teach that God is . . . not a real existence, but a figment of the human imagination, and that pure Buddhism is a better moral guide than Christianity." The founding of a Buddhist church and the arrival of Buddhist missionaries raised concerns for many Japanese Americans as well. They feared that this new presence would only serve to heighten the existing tensions with their American neighbors.

Their fears were soon realized. In 1906 San Francisco's school board voted to segregate Japanese students from their peers. In 1907 the United States persuaded Japan's government to stop allowing their citizens to come to this country, and the U.S. Immigration Act of 1924 officially forbade immigration from Japan and other nations sending "undesirable" immigrants. The California Alien Land Law of 1913 went a step farther by prohibiting all Chinese and Japanese immigrants from owning property. The law faced little political opposition, passing by a vote of thirty-five to two in the California Senate, and seventy-two to three in the Assembly. But even U.S. citizenship wasn't a guarantee that these "undesirables" could keep their property. During World War II, 110,000 residents of Japanese descent (a majority of them U.S. citizens) were sent to internment camps and forced to sell or abandon their homes and businesses. This series of events would have a lasting impact on the Japanese Buddhist religious community, both galvanizing it and forcing accommodation.

THE RELIGIOUS LANDSCAPE

Based on the numbers, the religious landscape of San Francisco is dominated by Roman Catholicism. Prominent Catholic churches are scattered across the area and 23 percent of the residents are members of a Roman Catholic church.

But San Francisco is well known for its spiritual nonconformity and experimentation. New age, hippie, countercultural—it is difficult to place a single label on this phenomenon. One author has called California a "theme park of the gods" featuring a "steady parade of utopian sects, bohemian mystics, cult leaders, psychospiritual healers, holy poets, sex magicians, fringe Christians, and psychedelic warriors." When the sociologists Rodney Stark and William Sims Bainbridge counted new religious movements (NRMs or cults) in the 1980s, they found that California was the headquarters and typically the founding location for 167 of these movements, more than twice the number in any other state.

These movements have often borrowed elements from the Asian traditions found in the city. In the 1960s, for example, San Francisco and other areas in California produced many communes frequently claiming a foundation in Buddhism, Hinduism, or other Asian traditions. And it has often been European Americans who participate in these hybrid or neo-Asian groups. This phenomenon is sometimes called "elite" religion, as the participants are often highly educated individuals attracted to the exotic or nontraditional nature of these traditions.

Zen Buddhism is probably the most popular example of "elite" religion in the United States. While Zen dates back many centuries in China and Japan, it has gained a significant following among Americans of European descent. In the 1950s there was a "Zen boom" as people were introduced to its ideas through the popular writings of people like Jack Kerouac and Alan Watts. In 1962 Suzuki Roshi founded the

A street in San Francisco's Chinatown. One of the oldest and largest Chinese communities in the United States, Chinatown is home to many Taoist and Buddhist temples.

San Francisco Zen Center. Today the center is one of the largest Buddhist congregations outside of Asia, and most of its members are non-Asians.

Most expressions of the Asian religions, however, are far more traditional and are more closely tied to a specific ethnic group. We identified several areas and many temples we wanted to visit. Our exploration of Buddhism and Taoism began in the most obvious of places: Chinatown.

San Francisco's Chinatown is the oldest Chinese enclave in the mainland United States and one of the largest Chinese neighborhoods outside of Asia. As we toured Chinatown, we found evidence of Taoism and Buddhism throughout the neighborhood, from the items sold in local shops to the many temples. These religions are not entirely exclusive, however, as individuals will often practice both traditions simultaneously. The religions themselves often overlap, with some deities being prominent in both. Indeed, many of the temples in Chinatown are explicitly labeled as "Buddhist and Taoist."

Initially, the temples were not easy to find. They are often located on the third floor of a building, with only a small sign above a staircase outside denoting their presence. In many cases a benevolent association or a *huiguan* is located on the second floor, immediately below the temple. Along with creating and supporting temples, these member-supported associations provide a wide variety of services, such as helping members with expenses for funerals and health care. They also serve as a collective voice for the city's Chinese population when interacting with politicians and other officials.

American Christians saw the Chinese community in San Francisco as a natural extension of their missionary work in mainland China. Evidence of these efforts remain in the form of several Chinese Christian churches and other similar organizations. The English lessons provided by these missionary organizations were often a central attraction for Chinese immigrants.

More prominent in their architecture, though fewer in number, are the Christian churches in Chinatown. Because news of the gold rush was first disseminated at major ports in China, where Protestant missionaries were active, many of the new immigrants were already Christian. This, combined with the substantial support of local Christian missions in San Francisco, meant that Christian churches were established quite early in Chinatown. For example, the First Chinese Baptist Church was established by the American Baptist Home Mission Society in 1888. The nearby Presbyterian Church in Chinatown was established even earlier, in 1853, and claims to be "America's first Chinese Church." Services are held in Mandarin, Cantonese, and English.

San Francisco also has a Japanese enclave, or Japan-town, although it is not as large as Chinatown. While Buddhism has been the primary religious tradition among Japanese immigrants in the United States, their congregations differ significantly in theology and style from the Buddhist temples found in Chinatown. In Chinatown one finds temples devoted to a mix of Taoism and Chinese forms of Buddhism, but the city's Japanese Buddhists primarily practice a strain of Buddhism known as Jodo Shinshu, a school of Pure Land Buddhism. Furthermore, while Chinese Buddhism in the United States tends to be decentralized, Japanese Buddhism here is structured around a denomination-like organization called the Buddhist Churches of America.

The presence and influence of these Asian traditions are not isolated in San Francisco's ethnic neighborhoods. As you travel around the city and nearby towns you are likely to see many churches, temples, meditation centers, monasteries, and other illustrations of the influence of Buddhism and other traditions. Some of these are simply extensions of what is found in the ethnic neighborhoods, others are Western adaptations of Asian traditions by non-Asian individuals, and still others are somewhere in between.

A unique example of the latter is the Dharma Realm Buddhist Association. In 1962 a Buddhist teacher named Xuan Hua moved to San Francisco with the goal of establishing Chinese Buddhism in the West, with an emphasis on the monastic lifestyle. To this end, Hua founded the Dharma Realm Buddhist Association, which now consists of several temples, monasteries, schools and a Buddhist University. Although many of these institutions serve mainly Chinese constituencies and are strongly rooted in Chinese Buddhism, large numbers of European American participants have been attracted to places like the Berkeley Buddhist Monastery.

THE RELIGIOUS EXPERIENCE

As we walked through Chinatown we came upon a sign above a staircase that said "Tin How Temple." Curious, we climbed the stairs. After some gentle redirecting by the second-floor residents, who were probably affiliated with the temple's benevolent society, we arrived at the temple on the third floor, and our senses became saturated. The smell of incense filled the air, bright colors billowed throughout the room, and a cool air flowed through the open side overlooking the street below.

In the center of the room was an altar overflowing with statues of deities. In the middle was a statue of Tin How, the Cantonese name for the goddess Mazu. Mazu is recognized in both Taoism and Buddhism as the goddess of the sea, who protects fishermen and others who venture out on the ocean. Like many of the other temples we visited in Chinatown, the Tin How Temple illustrated the fluid boundaries between Taoism and Buddhism. On the altar were a variety of offerings to the goddess, such as fruit, and large stone containers holding burning sticks of incense. Hanging from the ceiling were dozens of red lanterns with the names of individual

Temples in San Francisco's Chinatown are often located on the top floor of a building. Seen above is the entrance to the Tin How Temple.

devotees. While we were there, a woman entered, lighted incense, and began praying at the altar.

Susan Woon, who was overseeing the activities, explained that the temple receives donations for the services they provide and the items they sell. The paper lanterns hanging from the ceiling had been placed there by individual families to bring good luck. She grabbed a can of sticks and began shaking them to show us how fortunes were told. Once a stick fell from the can, she revealed a number on the stick and then went to a large rack to retrieve a fortune. In addition, they sold incense and other items for use in the temple.

Most of the small Taoist and Buddhist temples we visited in Chinatown were strikingly different from other religious congregations in the United States. They did not offer weekly religious services associated with a typical American Christian congregation. There were no sermons, nor was there a pastor or similar leader. Instead, these temples offer a place where individual worshipers can come to pray to a particular deity or deities and perform rituals.

Americans often think of and speak about the many different branches and types of Christianity but when it comes to Buddhism, Taoism, and other religious traditions, we often fail to perceive these same distinctions. There is a natural tendency to see more diversity among things that seem familiar and more homogeneity among that which is different or foreign to our everyday experience. But exploring San Francisco is one way to quickly appreciate the ethnic, historical, and theological differences found within Buddhism and many other religions.

The Tin How temple was similar to many Buddhist and Taoist temples in Chinatown, but the Buddhist Church of San Francisco in Japantown offered a completely new experience. Initially, this Buddhist Church seemed to have more in common with traditional Protestant churches than the Buddhist temples we had just visited. The building was called

The inside of the Tin How Temple in San Francisco's Chinatown. The temple is dedicated to a deity that is recognized in both Taoism and Buddhism. Individuals typically come to the temple to make offerings of incense to the temple's deity.

a church, the religious leaders were called ministers or reverends, and the congregation supported multiple social and sporting groups, including a long-standing Boy Scout troop. As we toured the offices and read the bulletin boards and newsletters, the similarities mounted.

Even the worship area and services held at the Buddhist Church of San Francisco had some similarities to a typical Protestant congregation. The worship area is furnished with wooden pews, with an aisle between the pews

The leader of the Buddhist Church of San Francisco, Reverend Ronald Kobata: "My main responsibility is to understand as best I can and share my appreciation of what the basic insights of a Buddhist's teachings can help to address suffering."

for processionals. On one side of the altar is a pulpit and on the other is a lectern and an organ. The worship service, which is held on Sundays, begins with the ringing of a bell, at which point the congregation has a period of quiet meditation. The congregation then collectively recites a sutra, or part of the Buddhist scriptures, after which the minister gives a dharma talk, which is much like a sermon and lasts about twenty minutes. This is followed by singing and general congregational announcements. When the service concludes, individuals go to the altar and light incense as an offering and then head to the social hall for tea and desserts.

Some of the differences between the Buddhist Church of San Francisco and the temples we visited in Chinatown can be explained by their affiliation with different branches of Buddhism. The Jodo-Shinshu school of Buddhism, commonly practiced in Japantown, places an emphasis on the

The worship area of the Buddhist Church of San Francisco. Although the congregation was established in 1898, its current building was built in 1935. Construction was motivated by the King of Siam (modern-day Thailand) who wanted to present relics of the Buddha to Buddhists in the United States. As a result, the new building features a room on its roof to contain the relics, called a stupa.

communal learning and practical application of the Buddha's teachings rather than private meditation. Other differences can be explained by variations in ethnicity, with the Chinatown temples exhibiting influences from Taoism and Chinese folk religions. But when asked about the similarities between Christian churches and the Buddhist Church of San Francisco, the leaders consistently stressed the unique pressure on the Japanese community to "Americanize" and blend into the culture following World War II. Elaine Donlin, the assistant pastor of the church told us, "it kind of drives me crazy—the comparisons to Christianity— because the tradition is night and day. However, we sure do look like it, we play organ music, we sing hymns." The resident minister, the Reverend Ronald Kobata, noted that in earlier decades there was "a concerted effort to develop a more Protestant image." He explained that weekly worship services are not a part of traditional Buddhism; instead, families are encouraged to have a home altar where they pray and perform ceremonies daily.

Kobata also described the period of transition that his congregation and its denomination are currently undergoing. He told us that when the Buddhist Churches of America was started by Japanese immigrants, "it pretty much stayed within the ethnic community, and I guess, for various reasons . . . the tradition has pretty much tried to stay within its . . . ethnic roots. But gradually because of more generations being more Americanized and so forth, we're able to articulate and present these traditions in English." Although he estimated that 80 percent of their congregation is of Japanese descent, many of the members, including Kobata, can no longer speak Japanese fluently (if at all), and none of his six assistants is of Japanese descent.

Kobata acknowledged that Jodo-Shinshu Buddhism is not receiving the attention Zen received in the 1950s, but he noted that they are in the "process of trying to become a more open tradition in America and developing our own identity." He shared an illustration to help us understand the challenges involved in this process. "I'd introduce myself and . . . they would say 'Oh, you're from that Japanese church.' I say 'No, no, no, no, it's not a Japanese church, it's a Buddhist temple.' It just happens that there are a lot of people of people of Japanese ancestry there, but Buddhism is not a Japanese religion, it's not an Asian religion, it's international, it's a universal spiritual appreciation.

Regardless of what your cultural background is, you should be able to appreciate it."

However, like all of the "immigrant" religious groups we have observed on our travels, the transition is a slow one, filled with generational and cultural compromises. Even universal religions and religious experiences acquire very specific rituals and routines, which are tightly interwoven with the local culture of the congregation.

BEYOND THE TEMPLE

As in the other locations we visited, the Asian religions of San Francisco have an impact that extends far beyond the city. San Francisco served as active port of entry for Asian religions in the late nineteenth century and remains the national hub for many of these groups today. The national headquarters for the Buddhist Church of America is located next to the Buddhist Church of San Francisco, their seminary is located across the bay in Berkeley, and as noted earlier, the San Francisco Zen Center, the Dharma Realm Buddhist centers, and many others are located in the area. Along with serving as organizational hubs, these centers and seminaries have made San Francisco an information hub for Buddhism, Taoism, and other Asian religions.

At a much more abstract level, Buddhism and other Asian religions have saturated the larger culture far beyond the presence of temples, seminaries, and national headquarters. When you sip "Zen" tea or speak of "karma" it reflects some of the broad diffusion of Asian religious practices and concepts into the language and culture of the United States. The influences are seen most directly in new religions, but the entire religious culture (including mainstream religions) has felt the influence of these religions. Some Christian groups are now exploring Buddhist teachings and history in greater depth. For example, the ecumenical Graduate Theological Union and the Berkeley Institute of Buddhist Studies now jointly offer a Master of Arts degree in Buddhist Studies.

But the larger culture has also shaped Asian religious communities. In San Francisco this has been most striking for Japanese Buddhists. Both historical accounts and our interviews with local ministers show that discrimination against Buddhists, and the Japanese immigrants more generally, was a powerful force in shaping their community. The hostility of the surrounding culture served to simultaneously strengthen the distinctive Japanese Buddhist identity and to force the community to Americanize.

When Japanese immigrants first began to arrive in the United States, they were hesitant to declare themselves Buddhists. No doubt many were never practicing Buddhists, but others were cautious of doing so in an overwhelmingly Christian nation. As laws were passed forbidding additional Japanese immigration and denying existing Japanese immigrants the right to own land, the immigrants soon turned to local Buddhist congregations for support. The Buddhist scholar Kenneth K. Tanaka explains that the exclusionary laws of the early twentieth century "turned out to be a windfall for the Buddhist temples . . . [which] came to be perceived as an ethnic refuge and bastion for Japanese culture amidst the sea of hostile society."

The defining moment arrived on February 19, 1942, when President Franklin Delano Roosevelt signed and issued Executive Order 9066, authorizing the internment of Japanese Americans. A historical diary of the Berkeley Higashi Honganji temple records a succinct account of the forced evacuation: "Berkeley received orders to evacuate on April 26. Every Japanese had to evacuate by May 1. . . . [M]embers were scattered through different Relocation Centers. After the war, the Church was issued a temporary shelter for the returnees."

Upon returning from internment, many Japanese-Americans turned to Buddhist institutions for help. Ronald Kobota and other Buddhist ministers noted that the Buddhist churches of the Bay Area were well known for providing shelter and support. Yet, at the very time when Buddhist temples were uniting Japanese Americans around their religion and culture, the temples were making efforts to look more American. The most noticeable was a change in vocabulary.

Following a series of meetings at an internment camp in Topaz, Utah, in 1944, and a later meeting in Salt Lake City, the name of the national organization was changed from North American Buddhist Mission to the current Buddhist Churches of America. This is also when the temples began to be called "churches" and the local congregations attempted to reduce hostility and suspicion by looking and sounding more American (i.e., Protestant). This Americanization remains a point of debate within the group, and members of the local Buddhist "churches" typically still refer to them as temples.

Whether the immigrant religious group is Japanese Buddhists, Iranian Muslims, Polish Catholics, Indian Hindus, Russian Jews, or any of the hundreds of other ethnic and minority religious groups, the local congregation often offers an organizational haven from the larger culture, a haven that simultaneously retains elements of their own distinctive culture as it acclimates members to the new one. But as fewer members of the Buddhist Churches of America are of Japanese descent, the place of Japanese culture in the local congregation is slowly fading. Buddhism is opening a new chapter and developing a new identity within San Francisco and the larger culture.

REFERENCES AND FURTHER READING

American Experience. *The Transcontinental Railroad*. Public Broadcasting Service. Film and website.

Berglund, Barbara. 2007. *Making San Francisco American: Cultural Frontiers in the Urban West, 1846–1906*. Lawrence: University of Kansas Press.

Chen, Yong. 2000. *Chinese San Francisco, 1850–1943: A Trans-Pacific Community*. Stanford: Stanford University Press.

Davis, Erik. 2006. *The Visionary State: A Journey through California's Spiritual Landscape*. San Francisco: Chronicle Books.

Ellis, John Tracy, ed. 1962. *Documents of American Catholic History*. Milwaukee: The Bruce Publishing Company.

Finke, Roger. 1989. "The Demographics of Religious Participation: An Ecological Approach, 1850–1980." *Journal for the Scientific Study of Religion* 28:45–58.

Hittell, John S. 1878. *A History of the City of San Francisco and Incidentally of the State of California*. San Francisco: A. L. Bancroft and Company.

Imai, Akinori, Ichiji Yanaba, Roger Yamashita, Masuji Fujii, Joseph Yatabe, and Tadashi Hikoyeda, eds. 1976. Berkeley Higashi Honganji, 1926–1976. Self-published.

Loo, Chalsa M. 1991. *Chinatown: Most Time, Hard Time*. New York: Praeger Publishers.

Melton, J. Gordon, and Constance Jones. 2009. "Reflections on Buddhist Demographics in America: An Initial Report on the First American Buddhist Census." Presented at the annual meeting of the Association for the Study of Religion Economics, and Culture, April 2–4, Washington, DC.

Miller, Timothy. 2000. *The 60s Communes: Hippies and Beyond*. Syracuse, NY: Syracuse University Press.

Needleman, Joseph. 2009. *The New Religions*. New York: Penguin Group.

Seager, Richard Hughes. 1999. *Buddhism in America*. New York: Columbia University Press.

Stark, Rodney, and William Sims Bainbridge. 1985. *The Future of Religion*. Berkeley: University of California Press.

Tanaka, Kenneth K. 1997. *Ocean: An Introduction to Jodo-Shinshu Buddhism in America*. Berkeley, CA: Wisdom Ocean Publications.

Williams, Peter. 2002. *America's Religions: From Their Origins to the Twenty-First Century*. Urbana: University of Illinois Press.

A full-sized statue of ISKCON's founder, A.C. Bhaktivedanta Swami Prabhupada sits in the Berkeley ISKCON temple.

Hare Krishnas

WHEN TOURING THE PLACES of faith in Berkeley, California, we couldn't resist stopping by the temple of the International Society for Krishna Consciousness.

The International Society for Krishna Consciousness is often formally abbreviated as ISKCON, but its members are most popularly known as "Hare Krishnas." Although ISKCON has theological and historical ties to India, the movement really began in the United States. Its founder, A. C. Bhaktivedanta Swami Prabhupada, came to the United States in 1965 to spread a strain of Hinduism focused on devotional activities, such as chanting. Once in the United States, however, Prabhupada began to teach a more universalistic view of God, arguing that the various artificial barriers between different religions should be overcome so that individuals can practice a "pure religion." The central activity of ISKCON devotees is the frequent chanting of "Hare Krishna, Hare Krishna; Krishna Krishna, Hare Hare, Hare Rama, Hare Rama; Rama Rama, Hare Hare." Hare, Krishna, and Rama are all words referring to aspects of Krishna, whom practitioners view as the ultimate form of God.

ISKCON is a well-known group despite its meager size. The group's notoriety is primarily a function of the evangelistic energy of its members. At its zenith, the group grew to more than 100,000 members and seemed ubiquitous in the most public places of America, especially airports. Sporting orange robes and shaved heads, they

Mahesvari Devi Dasi joined the ISKCON movement in the 1970s.

chanted, handed out literature, and spoke with anyone willing to listen. ISKCON's profile was raised in the 1970s and 1980s when it was part of a social panic concerning alleged "brainwashing cults."

The public profile of ISKCON has garnered the movement a certain status in popular culture. It also attracted the interest of various celebrities in the 1960s and 1970s, such as George Harrison of the Beatles, who helped support some of the group's activities in Britain.

The temple we visited was a large, white-brick building tucked away in a residential neighborhood of Berkeley. As we approached we

The Hare Krishna chant is the primary devotional activity of ISKCON adherents. The chant consists of three different names of what adherents believe to be the ultimate form of God.

saw two statues of Simhadvara the Lion, doorkeeper of New Jagannath Puri, one on each side of the giant glass front doors. We were greeted warmly by four women who were having lunch. They invited us to go into an adjoining room where we could view the deities. This was a large open room with high ceilings and altars for the deities on two of the walls. Each of the statues was adorned with flowers. As we moved to the next room we saw a group of women sewing flower garlands, which would later be placed on the deities.

We spoke with several members of the group, but the most vocal was Mahesvari Devi Dasi. She became a member of the group with her husband back in the early 1970s. She has remained active, but her husband is no longer a member. She said that when the group was first formed, nearly everyone lived on the site, often in very simple conditions. Despite being a Hare Krishna, she said that she still believes in Jesus, says the rosary, and holds fast to other Christian beliefs. For her the Krishna beliefs helped to explain more about God, what he looks like, what he does, and how she could get closer to him.

Although she acknowledged that many of the practices and teachings were similar to those of Hinduism, Mahesvari said that they do not limit themselves to Hinduism. This idea corresponds to Prabhupada's teachings that all religions have different names for the same God. In a conversation with a Christian, Prabhupada argued that "Christ is another way of saying Krsta and Krsta is another way of pronouncing Krishna, the name of God . . . it doesn't matter—Krishna or Christ—the name is the same. The main point is to follow the injunctions of the Vedic scriptures that recommend chanting the name of God in this age."

REFERENCES AND FURTHER READING

Bainbridge, William Sims. 1997. *The Sociology of Religious Movements.* New York: Routledge.

Rochford, E. Burke Jr. 1991. *Hare Krishna in America.* New Brunswick, NJ: Rutgers University Press.

SALT LAKE CITY, UTAH

No place in the United States is as strongly associated with a particular religion as Utah is with the Mormon Church—officially, the Church of Jesus Christ of Latter-day Saints (LDS). Indeed, a game of word association would likely show that the name "Utah" immediately evokes a response of "Mormon" from many individuals. There are more than four million Mormons in the United States, about one-third of them in Utah, where Mormons make up more than two-thirds of the population.

Our drive from Colorado Springs to the Salt Lake Valley took only a day. The majestic mountains remained an ever-present part of the scenery, but the religious geography underwent a complete transformation. Heading north on Interstate 15 we visited Provo (home of Brigham Young University), Salt Lake City (home of the LDS headquarters and Temple Square), Ogden and the many rapidly-growing towns

A statue of Brigham Young at Temple Square in Salt Lake City. Young led the Latter-day Saints westward until, upon seeing the Salt Lake Valley, he declared "This is the Place."

in between. This eighty-plus mile stretch of I-15 between Ogden and Salt Lake City cuts through four counties that are home to 76 percent of Utah's population and 75 percent of the state's Mormons. Utah County, the most southern of the four counties and the home of Provo, holds the highest concentration. Nearly nine out of ten residents are Mormon (88 percent). Interestingly, the county that includes Salt Lake City is actually among the least Mormon parts of Utah. Yet, even there, 56 percent of the population belongs to the LDS Church.

The Great Salt Lake is the heartland of Mormonism. This is the valley that the early Mormon leader, Brigham Young, first told his followers that this would be their new home. "This is the place," he declared. This proclamation is heard often in Utah and celebrated in the new state song: "Utah, This is the Place":

It was Brigham Young who led the pioneers across the
    plains,
They suffered with the trials they had to face.
With faith they kept on going
till they reached the Great Salt Lake.
Here they heard the words . . .
THIS IS THE PLACE!

THE HISTORY

Despite the strong connection between Mormons and "this place," the story of the largest "American-born" religion actually begins more than 2,000 miles away in Western New York. In 1820 Joseph Smith received a vision, in which two heavenly beings told him not to participate in the various religious groups and movements surrounding him at the time. He was fourteen years old. Three years later Smith had another vision in which he encountered the Angel Moroni. Smith said that the angel told him of an ancient population, descended from the Hebrews, who had inhabited America. The history of these people and

"This Is The Place Heritage Park" in Salt Lake City. In the foreground is a replica of a hand-cart that some Mormon settlers who could not afford an ox or horse used to transport their families and belongings. These settlers would physically pull these carts for the entire journey. The hand-cart has become an important symbol of Mormon determination.

their destruction was said to be contained in inscriptions on golden plates. Smith is said to have received these plates and the means to translate them in 1827. These inscriptions would become the Book of Mormon.

The Book of Mormon and Smith's other prophecies contained historical and theological themes from Old and New Testament Christianity, along with entirely unique material, and this created the tension that persists today. Mormonism has distinctive doctrines, but Mormons see themselves as Christian. Many traditional Christians, however, disagree. And so a debate has long raged over whether Mormonism is a Christian denomination or an entirely different religion.

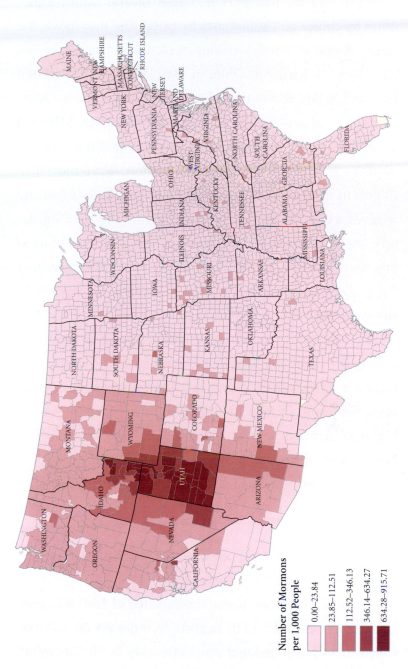

Number of Mormons per 1,000 People

- 0.00–23.84
- 23.85–112.51
- 112.52–346.13
- 346.14–634.27
- 634.28–915.71

The Mormon population. Although Latter-day Saints have a relatively significant presence in most of the West, nothing compares to their share of the population in Utah. In much of the state Mormons comprise over 70 percent of the population. (Data Source: Religious Congregations and Membership Study.)

Smith and his followers relocated several times, sometimes by choice and sometimes by force. The first move, the result of one of Smith's visions, took them from Palmyra, New York, to Kirtland, Ohio, in 1831. After Smith declared Jackson County, Missouri, to be the destined home for Mormons, several settlements were created along the Missouri River. Eventually, they were forced from their Missouri communities by the non-Mormon population. They moved to Illinois in 1839, where the group bought land in Nauvoo and received a charter for the community from the state legislature. Smith, who served as mayor of the town, drew the ire of the non-Mormon population, particularly after shutting down a newspaper that criticized Mormons. He was put in jail, and a mob later killed him and his brother.

The Mormons then chose Brigham Young as their new leader. The conflict and violence leading up to his appointment made it clear to Young that the Mormons needed to move yet again. In 1846 the first groups of Mormon settlers began to arrive in the Salt Lake Valley. They continued to flow into the area, which they had deemed isolated enough to provide them both peace and privacy. The Mormons called their new territory the "State of Deseret," a term meaning "honeybee" in the Book of Mormon. The U.S. government agreed to designate the area as the Utah Territory and appointed Brigham Young governor.

Although their new home was isolated at first, this soon changed as new railroad lines brought more people to Utah. Consequently, this brought more attention to the Mormons, including their practice of polygamy. The issue of polygamy became the focal point of conflict between the church and the federal government. It came to a head in 1890 after LDS president Wilford Wilson issued a statement encouraging Mormons to refrain from plural marriages. This change in Mormon practice opened the way for Utah to gain statehood in 1896.

THE RELIGIOUS LANDSCAPE

While statehood may have meant the end of official Mormon administration over Utah, the influence of Utah's religious roots remains. If you look closely, symbols of Mormon history and theology are found everywhere. The state bird, for instance, is the seagull. Legend has it that the Mormons' first crop in Utah was plagued by cricketlike insects, but seagulls miraculously appeared and devoured the horde.

Similarly, the beehive, which is a symbol of the Mormon Church, is included on the state seal, the state flag, and on

A panoramic photograph of downtown Salt Lake City in 1912. You can see the Mormon Temple (middle) and the Tabernacle (domed building to the right of the Temple). (Library of Congress, Prints and Photographs Division.)

road signs. Moreover, the state's nickname remains the "Beehive State," and the bee is Utah's official state insect and the mascot of their minor league baseball team. Utah also has a distinctive state holiday, celebrated on July 24, to commemorate the arrival of Brigham Young and the Mormon immigrants. Although officially called Pioneer Days, which might be considered generic enough to apply to all Utahans, the holiday is inescapably wrapped in Mormon history and identity.

Words from the Mormon lexicon, like "Deseret" and "Zion," are also common in the names of prominent Utah businesses. Some of these businesses have no current affiliation with the church (e.g., Zion Bank). Others are organized for LDS members (e.g., the Deseret First Credit Union). Still others provide direct services for the church's members (e.g., the LDS Employment Resource Services). In addition, the LDS Church has a "for profit" arm, the Deseret Management Corporation, which owns the *Deseret News*, Zion's Securities Corporation, and other Utah businesses. Because this corporation's board of directors is composed of the key leaders of the LDS Church, the church holds considerable sway in the state's business community. Both the formal and informal ties between the church and the local economy remain strong.

Despite the many Mormon symbols and names scattered throughout Utah, the most visible images of Mormon influence in Salt Lake City are the physical manifestations of the church seen in various buildings around the city. The LDS Church owns property in many areas of Salt Lake City, particularly in downtown, which is home to the

Symbols and words from Mormon theology and history are omnipresent in Salt Lake City. Seagulls, bees, beehives, "Zion," and "Deseret" are common on signs around the city. Above, the headquarters of the LDS-owned *Deseret News*, a Salt Lake newspaper. To the near right, the home of Salt Lake's minor league baseball team, the Bees. To the far right, the Utah State Highway signs feature beehives.

church's headquarters. It is common to see groups of missionaries and other LDS members walking around downtown as they attend conferences and other church functions. The General Conference of the LDS Church is held in the 21,000-seat Conference Center downtown, built in 2000.

Salt Lake City contains more than the administrative headquarters for Mormons, though. There are many buildings of immense theological importance as well, particularly in Temple Square. The most notable of these is the Salt Lake Temple itself. Temples are not "churches" in the typical sense of the word. They are not where Mormons go for weekly worship services. Instead, temples are designated for particularly special ceremonies, including weddings between two LDS members, assuming they are both in good standing with the church. The temples are not open to the public once they are officially dedicated (there are open houses when a temple is first constructed).

The Salt Lake Temple was the first temple founded after the Mormon immigration to Utah, and it is still the largest. Ground was broken by Brigham Young in 1853. The building was officially dedicated in 1893 (because it took forty years to build, it was actually the fourth temple *completed* in Utah). In addition to the complexity of the building, part of the delay in construction was due to the transportation of enormous blocks of granite-like stones by oxcart to the site from a quarry more than twenty miles away.

The temple is the theological center of Mormon life. Many cities in Utah, including Salt Lake City, are organized around

Above right, the laying of the capstone of the Salt Lake City Temple in 1892. Construction began in 1853 and was completed in 1893. (Library of Congress, Prints and Photographs Division, Historic American Buildings Survey).

Above left, the Salt Lake City Temple today. It is the largest Temple in the world. The gold statue at the top of the Temple depicts the Angel Moroni, who is said to have revealed the Mormon faith to Joseph Smith.

their temple. Even the roads are numbered based on their distance from the temple. For instance, if you are on 600 East and 1200 South, then you know that you are six blocks east and twelve blocks south of the temple. This makes getting around town easy. It also serves as a constant reminder of the city's historical and theological origins.

There are many resources to help a visitor learn about Mormon history and theology in Temple Square, but someone with a careful eye can pick up on many themes just by walking around. For instance, if you spend an hour in a shopping mall dodging armadas of strollers, you will quickly come to realize that Utah is a perpetual bull market for weddings and baby showers. Indeed, Utah has the nation's highest percentage of households containing married couples with children. The state also reports the highest percentage of the population under eighteen years of age.

Mormons place a strong emphasis on marriage and family. This includes strong social norms encouraging early marriage, having many children, "traditional" gender roles, and social sanctions against divorce. A trip to Brigham Young University in Provo, the flagship university of the LDS Church, can provide a person some appreciation for these features of Mormon life. The university publishes an official "Bridal Guide," which is distributed in the student union building. The university also specifies whether student parking lots include the *spouses* of students.

The emphasis on families is not simply a matter of morality but is based on unique theological underpinnings. Mormons, for instance, believe in "celestial marriages" that continue beyond death, assuming several requirements, including a ceremony in a temple, are fulfilled. Similarly, Mormons have a passion for studying family histories, or genealogies. Because many Mormons' ancestors had long been dead when Joseph Smith received his prophecies, living Mormons work to "baptize" these ancestors through temple ceremonies. These ancestors, however, must first be identified. As a result, the LDS church has built some of the largest genealogical archives and resources in the world, which they allow nonmembers to use.

A sign prohibiting parking for students *or student spouses,* a specification not likely required on many campuses in the United States. Given their religion's emphasis on families, Mormons tend to marry younger than their non-Mormon peers. Since over 25 percent of its students are married, Brigham Young University offers marriage counseling. In 2005 the campus newspaper reported that over fifty percent of BYU's students are married upon graduation.

In addition to the conspicuous presence of family-oriented stores and advertisements in Utah, you will likely notice the presence of another Mormon-driven industry. For instance, a billboard off one interstate advertises "missionary tested" suits for men. Another store offers sales on washable ties and other supplies for missionaries. Many religious groups have

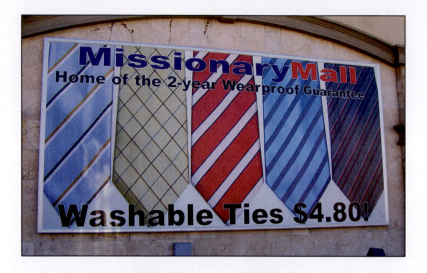

Missionary Mall in Provo, Utah. The missionary program is a central component of a Mormon's upbringing, especially for men. Men are strongly encouraged to serve for a two-year period once they turn 19 years of age. Women typically serve on 18-month missions and must be 21 years of age.

missionary programs. However, as is their style in most endeavors, the Mormons have created a missionary program that is bigger, more organized, and more extensive than any other. About 50,000 LDS missionaries are in the field at any one time. Most are men and women in their early twenties, although the men greatly outnumber women. Mormon missionaries typically serve a period of two years in an assigned location, often in another country.

Before they are sent to their field location, missionaries spend time at the Missionary Training Center where they learn a foreign language, if necessary, as well as general skills in presenting their faith to others. Training can last from one month to three months. The main center is located in Provo.

Because the trainees live at the center during this period, family members often send letters and care packages to them. In fact, there are delivery companies in the Salt Lake Area specifically serving the missionary market.

Long before the young men and women officially enter the training center, they receive extensive education and support for their missions. The LDS Church has built Mormon "seminaries" near each of the public high schools in Provo, Ogden, and Salt Lake City. Owned and operated by the church, these seminaries are staffed by teachers trained at the LDS Seminary and Institute of Religion. Beginning in the ninth grade, students are given "release time" during the school day to attend the seminary and study Mormon teachings and doctrine in greater depth. Even before high school, many Mormon families begin mission funds for their children, and congregations promote the merits of mission work.

THE RELIGIOUS EXPERIENCE

Given that Mormons are known for actively seeking conversations with non-Mormons, we thought interviewing a local religious leader would be easy. We quickly learned, however, that requesting a formal interview for a book is something entirely different than chatting with a local missionary or bishop. After a series of emails and a phone interview with a staff member in the LDS Media Relations office, we were eventually granted permission to interview Bishop Spencer

Smith of the Washington Terrace Ninth Ward, as well as the stake president who appointed him, Jeff Stevens.

Mormons call the local congregation a *ward*, and a collection of wards is called a *stake*. A stake is similar to a diocese, district, or presbytery in other religious traditions. The leader of the local congregation or ward is called a *bishop*, and the leader of the stake is called the *stake president*, not to be confused with the worldwide LDS Church president. Thus, our conversations with Bishop Smith and President Stevens gave us a window into the life of local Mormon congregations. Despite the initial challenges of getting permission from the central office, our conversations were cordial and candid.

The Ninth Ward is located in Washington Terrace, a small town near Ogden with neatly kept lawns and 1970s-era homes. The average age of residents is higher than in Utah as a whole (30.6 compared to 27.1), yet still far lower than the national average (35.3). Because well over half of the local population is Mormon, the 300-plus members of the Ninth Ward all reside within a relatively small neighborhood.

Like all Mormon bishops and stake presidents, Bishop Smith and President Stevens are not paid. Smith manages multiple Subway sandwich shops in the area, and Stevens is an assistant superintendent of the local school district. They estimate that the average Mormon bishop devotes a minimum of twenty hours per week to his duties, and some weeks twice that. A bishop's tenure typically runs about five to seven years, depending on the decision of the stake president. After serving, a bishop usually returns to another position in the ward. President Stevens shared the story of a man in his stake who served as bishop one year and was an assistant in the nursery the next. This is a leadership path that Bishop Smith aspires to follow, but he would prefer to be an assistant in the children's Sunday school.

If the bishops are the most visible volunteers in the local congregation, they are not alone. Each ward has between 150 and 250 volunteer positions. These positions, including everything from Sunday school and worship to social groups and scouting, are considered "callings" from God rather than from the bishop. Given that the average ward has about 400 members, nearly all active members have a "calling" and are required to give of their time. But the volunteering goes beyond the local ward to include the mission activities mentioned earlier, as well as duties at Mormon agencies and temples. The temple in Salt Lake City alone has well over 1,000 volunteers.

Considering that Mormons are expected to give generously of time and money, and they pay no salaries to their leaders, it would seem a given that the local congregation would invest heavily in facilities. Yet not only are the facilities comparatively modest, the Ninth Ward shares its building with two other congregations as well as the stake office. When asked how three different congregations and an administrative office could agree on design and decorations for a single meeting house, they explained that most of the decisions are made by "Salt Lake." Bishop Smith said that he could decorate his office, but when it comes to the hallways and worship area, everything is standardized.

Wearing his Brigham Young University (BYU) tie, Bishop Spencer Smith stands in front of a neighborhood map of the 9th Ward detailing which homes are occupied by Mormon families.

Perhaps the greatest challenge is coordinating activities on Sunday. Each congregation has more than three hours of Sunday activities to plan, many of them focused on children; so Sunday becomes a well-orchestrated event. To make things easier, the wards alternate their starting times each month, with one ward beginning at 9 a.m., a second at 11 a.m., and a third at 1 p.m. Yet, even with the staggered starting times, overlap remains.

On the Sunday we visited, the Ninth Ward began its activities at 1 p.m., just as another ward was preparing to begin worship. The first hour was devoted to the societies and organizations within the ward. Men attend priesthood meetings,

Bishop Spencer Smith and Stake President Jeff Stevens review the long list of volunteer positions (callings) in the local ward.

the women go to the Relief Society, and the children attend religious education classes called Primary. The young men's group we attended shared ideas on how to prepare children for temple activities and a mission, and how to combat the secular influences around them. The second hour was devoted to more formal instruction for all ages. The adult class read and discussed teachings from the Book of Mormon. Finally, the third hour was devoted to worship.

On many Sundays the worship service resembles that of many Protestants, sometimes even using the same hymns. But this was the first Sunday of the month, which is known as Fast and Testimony Sunday. Rather than having a bishop or another leader give a message, members are invited to come forward and give their testimonies midway through the service.

Outside the Washington Terrace Ninth Ward before the worship service.

Women and men of all ages gave testimonies, though the women far outnumbered the men. Young mothers expressed thanks for help they had received from others in the ward. Several older adults spoke about the joy of temple work, and people of all ages talked about the blessing of family. Four children under the age of twelve and two teenage girls gave brief testimonies on their love of family and the church. Although the testimonies covered many topics, nearly all included variations of the following: a testimony on the truth of the church and Joseph Smith's visions (or the Book of Mormon), thanksgiving for the modern-day prophet (the LDS president), expressions of love and thanks for their family, the local ward and the church, and a statement on receiving salvation through Jesus Christ. A box of tissues was placed next to the lectern in anticipation of emotional testimonies. Once the testimonies were complete, the service closed with another hymn and a blessing. The worship ended shortly after 4 p.m. From well before 9 a.m. to well after 4 p.m., this Mormon meeting house truly was a beehive of activity.

BEYOND THE WARD

Given the impact that Mormon theology and history have on the culture of Utah, the distinctiveness of the group's beliefs and practices, along with the overall lingering suspicions and negative attitudes toward Mormons in the United States, we should probably not be surprised at the presence of a strong non-Mormon counterculture in Salt Lake. Indeed, almost half of Salt Lake's county is not Mormon, and the city is becoming steadily less Mormon as time passes. Still, there is some irony, you might even say tragic irony, that the place that was supposed to serve as a safe haven for Mormons produces its own hostilities toward the group. The LDS Church actively works to dispel negative perceptions of their faith in Salt Lake and throughout the world, although some of these perceptions are clearly rooted in the actual historical or contemporary practices of the church.

A coffee shop in Salt Lake City. The LDS church prohibits the ingestion of coffee and other stimulants. The term "Jack Mormon" is used to refer to a Mormon who does not practice the faith to the highest standard. Hence, a Mormon patronizing this particular shop is likely a "Jack Mormon."

Strong reactions to Mormon dominance in Utah come from both secular and religious rivals. They disagree on what they would like to see changed. Secular rivals oppose the church's conservative stances on moral issues. Conservative religious groups oppose what they view as heretical religious teachings. Both groups agree that the dominance of Mormonism has made them feel like outsiders. They note that the church is a powerful force at every level of politics and suggest that nothing is decided in Utah politics without permission from the "head shed" (i.e., LDS headquarters).

Others claim that Mormons hold a favored position in everything from employment to education. One of the chief complaints of the religious minority is the strong pressures their children face to become Mormon. They complain that the Mormon culture permeates virtually all institutions, from scouting groups and athletic clubs to the local public schools. As teens enter high school, the boundaries become especially sharp as Mormon membership determines attendance at the nearby seminary as well as the potential dating pool. Both religious schools and charter schools offer alternatives to the public schools.

Even though the rivalries can be bitter at times, many of the tensions are a source of satire and humor. Because the church opposes the drinking of alcohol and caffeine—all caffeine and alcoholic beverages are banned from BYU's campus—the cultural outsiders often incorporate Mormon lingo and themes into their drinks. The sign "Jack Mormon Coffee Co." and its slogan "this is the place (for fresh roasted coffee beans)" might mean little to visitors, but the natives know that Jack Mormons are lapsed or inactive Mormons. The line "this is the place" is rooted in Brigham Young's famous pronouncement about Utah. Beers get even more creative with their names and logos. Even though it has now been more than a century since the mainstream of Mormonism encouraged polygamy, the target of Wasatch Brewery's "Polygamy Porter" beer is clear.

REFERENCES AND FURTHER READING

Givens, Terryl. 2007. *People of Paradox: A History of Mormon Culture.* Oxford: Oxford University Press.

Hinton, Wayne K. 2000. *Utah: Unusual Beginning to Unique Present.* Sun Valley, CA: American Historical Press.

May, Dean L. 1987. *Utah: A People's History*. Salt Lake City: University of Utah Press.

Schaefer, Richard T., and William W. Zellner. 2008. "The Mormons" in *Extraordinary Groups: An Examination of Unconventional Lifestyles*. New York: Worth Publishers.

Wharton, Tom. 1995. *Utah*. Oakland, CA: Compass American Guides.

Williams, Peter W. 2002. "Mormons and the 'Mainstream.'" In *America's Religions: From Their Origins to the Twenty-First Century*. Urbana: University of Illinois Press.

Our Lady of Peace Shrine

As we approached the Nebraska border from Wyoming, we began to see something on the horizon. Surely, we thought, that can *not* be a huge religious shrine over there, in the middle of this sparse landscape? We quickly exited the highway to investigate further. Despite our original surprise, what we found near Pine Bluffs, Wyoming (population around 1,200), was the Our Lady of Peace Shrine. Standing at more than thirty feet tall, the 180-ton cast-marble figure is one of the largest statues of the Virgin Mary in the United States.

Created in 1998, the Our Lady of Peace Shrine was the result of a seven-year effort by one Roman Catholic couple, Ted and Marjorie Trefren. The couple used their savings and raised funds to pay for the $400,000 shrine. They were motivated to create the sculpture after taking a trip in 1991 to Europe and seeing shrines to the Virgin Mary in France and Yugoslavia. They returned with a desire that their home state of Wyoming have its own shrine. The flat, five-acre location near the I-80 highway was ideal because it was visible to those driving by and it was handicap-accessible.

More than two hundred people attended the dedication of the shrine in June 1999. Ted Trefren died a few years after the shrine was completed, and Marjorie now maintains the site with the help of her five sons and two daughters. She and all of her children live in Cheyenne, Wyoming, a thirty-nine-mile drive from the shrine. When we asked about starting an endowment for supporting the shrine, she

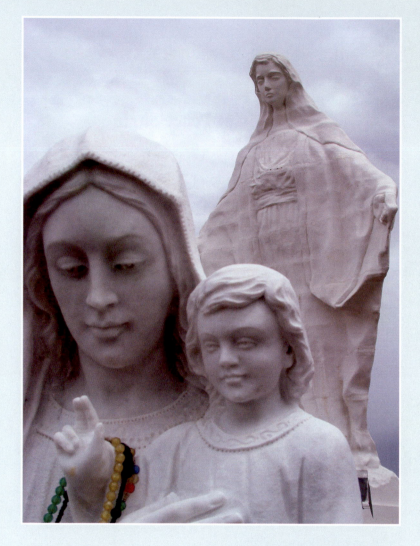

The main statue of Mary in the background is on a 10-foot pedestal and stands 30 feet on its own.

said it was not really needed. Marjorie explained that when money is needed, the Lord provides another donation. When we asked about vandalism, she said that the harsh weather was the only vandal. The family invites visitors to sign their guest book, and they have now

The white marble of the Our Lady of Peace Shrine contrasts with approaching storm clouds near the Wyoming-Nebraska border. Dedicated in 1999, the shrine was the brainchild of a former railroad worker and his wife. The actual sculpture was created by a Wyoming artist.

gone through many books. Marjorie told us that people come from "everywhere," and she assured us that she faithfully reads everything they write.

Several additions now surround the towering centerpiece including a variety of smaller statues, benches, and memorials. At least once a year, usually at the end of June, the local Catholic bishop holds a Mass at the shrine. Marjorie Trefren told a local newspaper, "this is not just for Catholics—it's for people. . . . We hope it will get people to pray again, and realize there is more to life." The handwritten messages, flowers, and other items left by at the shrine seem to show that visitors are fulfilling the Trefrens' vision.

REFERENCES AND FURTHER READING

Kelly, Guy. June 20, 1998. "Virgin Mary Statue on I-80 Ends 7-Year Quest."
Rocky Mountain News.

Eastwood, Cara. April 10, 2005. "Old World Tour Inspires Woman to Build
    Shrine." *Wyoming Tribune-Eagle.*
Glover, Paula. June 15, 1998. "Our Lady of Peace Shrine to be Unveiled."
    Wyoming Tribune-Eagle.
———. June 5, 1999. "Our Lady of Peace Shrine Nearly Ready for Dedica-
    tion." *Wyoming Tribune-Eagle.*
———. June 13, 1999. "Shrine Dedication." *Wyoming Tribune-Eagle.*

SIX

CENTRAL NEBRASKA

Many of the places we visited were urban. There are indeed interesting stories to be found in the big cities with their large, diverse, and often changing populations. Rural America, on the other hand, is idealized by some and criticized by others as being homogenous and frozen in time. But religion in rural America is not without its unique characteristics nor is it isolated from many of the same social forces shaping the suburbs and cities. This became clear as we spent time in the small towns of central Nebraska.

Lacking natural wonders or major cities to attract tourists, Nebraska often goes unexplored and largely unnoticed. For some, this state is a nondescript "flyover state." For others, it is 455 grueling miles of I-80. Yet, once you exit the Interstate, tour the countryside, and visit the small towns, the charm of rural living and a wealth of stories soon emerge. In Nebraska we discovered the often unappreciated story of how religion and ethnicity shaped the identity of small rural towns, and how they continue to alter these towns today.

A statue stands in a field near Our Lady of Mt. Carmel Catholic church in Paplin, Nebraska.

Whereas the religious narrative of Utah was the story of Mormonism, the Nebraska plains were seasoned with a diverse array of European religious and ethnic groups at the end of the nineteenth century. Today, a new wave of Hispanic immigrants is arriving.

We toured the communities of Grand Island, Ravenna, and a host of small villages surrounding them. Whereas the eastern portion of the state has two "major" cities, Lincoln (pop. 226,062) and Omaha (pop. 373,215), as you head west the population thins and the distance between small towns increases. Grand Island (pop. 42,940) serves as a hub for central Nebraska, and its commercial industries, especially the large meatpacking plants, have attracted a recent wave of Hispanic immigrants. The small town of Ravenna (pop. 1,341) lies an additional thirty-three miles west, nearing the desolate Sand Hills area. And, though Ravenna might seem small to many an outsider, it is far larger than the small towns surrounding it.

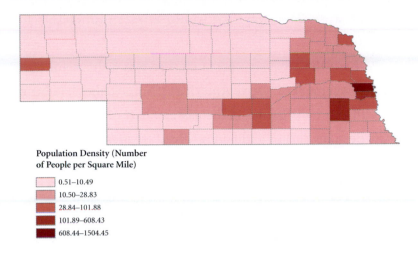

Population Density (Number of People per Square Mile)

	0.51–10.49
	10.50–28.83
	28.84–101.88
	101.89–608.43
	608.44–1504.45

Outside of a few counties in the eastern part of the state, much of Nebraska is very sparsely populated. As seen in this map, most of the counties in the central and western parts of the state have fewer than five people per square mile. These rural areas have active communities of faith, but they face unique challenges when it comes to basic issues such as maintaining enough support for a place of worship and finding a leader for a congregation. (Data Source: United States Census Bureau.)

THE HISTORY

Nebraska's broad, flat Platte River Valley was a thoroughfare to the West in the mid-1800s. Settlers followed the valley on their way to Oregon, Mormons trekked the valley as they emigrated to Utah, and when gold was found in California, the valley became a well-traveled route for the 49ers and other fortune-seekers who followed. From 1849 to 1854 an estimated 220,000 travelers went through Nebraska. Yet in 1854, at the time of the Kansas-Nebraska Act, a census found only 2,732 residents who were not Native Americans, and even this count is probably high. Despite this lack of settlers, changes were underway that would attract immigrants to the plains.

Perhaps the most significant change was a shameful one: the displacement of Native Americans. Some tribes had been forced from their homes in the eastern part of the state only a few decades earlier and had received treaties guaranteeing the new land in perpetuity. They soon learned the limits of perpetuity. By the 1840s many of the tribes of eastern and central Nebraska had ceded their land, and by the late 1850s nearly all were gone. The western tribes fought on, but the arrival of railroads, in general, and more specifically the completion of the transcontinental railroad in 1869, resulted in their defeat. The door for new settlements in Nebraska was opened.

Not only did the new railroads carry freight and people to the desolate prairies, they actively promoted the settling of Nebraska to Europeans. Receiving nearly 17 percent of the total Nebraska acreage from the U.S. government, including much of the very best farmland, the railroads sold large tracts of land to companies that were targeting buyers from specific countries and religious groups. Roman Catholics and Lutherans, in particular, took the lead in colonizing the new lands. Often criticized for sending the faithful to the godless frontier, Bishop John Ireland reminded fellow Catholics that "man made the city, but God made the country." Along with the cheap railroad land, the 1862 Homestead Act offered up to 160 acres of Nebraska's public land for free, if the new resident would till the soil for five years or more. Together these new developments helped grow Nebraska's population to

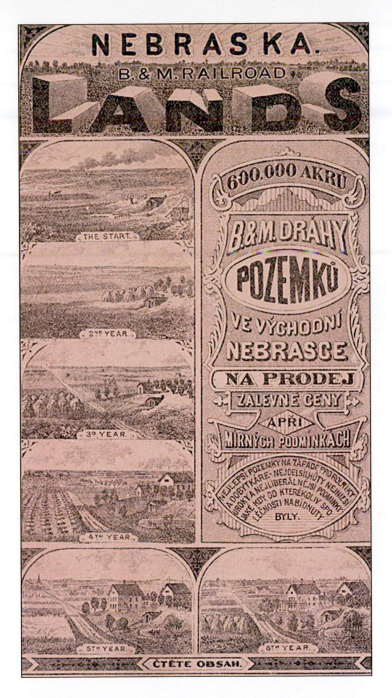

A poster from the 19th century produced by B. & M. Railroad encourages Czech immigrants to settle in Nebraska. The panels show the anticipated improvement in a Nebraska farm after six years of cultivating the land. The text states that Nebraska offers "the best land in the West" at "discount prices." (Courtesy of the Nebraska State Historical Society.)

122,993 by 1870 and more than one million by 1890. The bulk of these new residents were from foreign lands.

By 1870 European immigrants and their children dominated the counties we were exploring. Nearly one-half of the population was foreign-born, and more than 71 percent (942) had two foreign-born parents. Given that less than 28 percent of the foreign-born population was from an English-speaking country, a language other than English was spoken in at least half of the homes in the area that became Hall, Howard, and Buffalo counties. Even as late as 1890, by which time immigration had greatly slowed, 44 percent (21,359) of the residents in these counties had foreign-born parents. But as the free and cheap land of the new frontier became settled and economic development slowed, the flow of immigrants dropped sharply by the close of the nineteenth century.

A century after the rush of immigrants began, there were few foreign-born residents to be found in Nebraska. Only 1

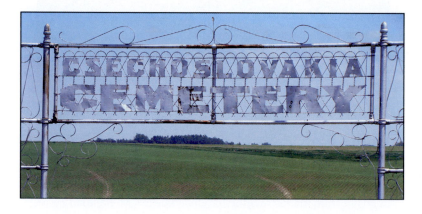

A sign marking the entrance to a Czechoslovakian cemetery in central Nebraska.

percent of the residents in these central Nebraska counties were foreign-born in 1970. But by 1990, a few new immigrants started to appear in Hall County, and the percentage of foreign-born edged up to 2 percent. This percentage increased to 8.3 in 2000 and was estimated at 11.3 in 2006. Not only did the volume of the flow change, but so did its source. Two-thirds of the new immigrants were from Central America, and by 2006, 18 percent of Hall County was Hispanic. The old immigrants from Europe remain the clear majority, but the recent immigrants are redefining the local religious landscape.

For each wave of immigration, whether past or present, local congregations have served as safe havens for preserving ethnicity, language, and unique expressions of religion. We begin our exploration by touring some of these old ethnic havens in the countryside.

THE RELIGIOUS LANDSCAPE

Because many small towns in Nebraska were settled predominantly by people of one European nationality, their annual community celebrations often reflect this ethnic identity. Czech communities are especially celebratory of their heritage, and seemingly everything else. Wilber, a town of 1,729 residents, holds an annual Czech Festival that attracts more than 50,000 visitors. It also hosts the Miss Czech-Slovak U.S. Pageant. But Wilbur isn't alone in celebrating its ancestry. Other small towns have German, Swedish, Norwegian, Irish, Polish, and other

Two men having a conversation in the center of Dannebrog, Nebraska during its Danish Constitution Festival. A sign at the entrance to town notes that it is the "Danish Capital of Nebraska."

ethnic festivals. When we arrived in Grand Island, we learned that Dannebrog (pop. 352), a town about twenty-three miles to the northwest and claiming to be the "Danish Capital of Nebraska," was celebrating their annual Grundlovs Fest (the Danish Constitution Festival). This festival seemed like the perfect excuse to take a trip to explore small towns and rural churches.

By central Nebraska standards, our road trip was a brief one. We took a seventy-five-mile loop and never strayed more than thirty miles north of Grand Island. Yet, this short tour introduced us to the rich ethnic and religious variation in the Nebraska countryside. The day began with an early lunch at the Grundlovs Fest in Dannebrog. Sad to say, we missed cow bingo, but we did have a chance to try Aebleskiver

(Danish pancakes). We also found plenty of people willing to tell their stories about Dannebrog and the history of the local churches. Even without the stories, it was impossible to ignore that this town was proud of being Danish. From village signs to the names of businesses, its heritage was proudly displayed. Indeed, Dannebrog is the name of the Danish flag.

The story of this Danish settlement begins when the Danish Land and Homestead Company of Milwaukee purchased a large tract of land in 1871. Danish settlers soon followed and, by 1872, Danish Lutheran pastors were preaching in Dannebrog. By 1874 a pastor was living there. Around 1883 disputes within the congregation resulted in the founding of St. Peder's Danish Lutheran church in Nysted, a small settlement five miles away. Despite the disputes over church doctrine and practices, however, there was no dispute about ethnicity. Danish was the only language spoken in Dannebrog's Our Saviour's Lutheran congregation until 1918. English was first used in Sunday school classes for children, and by 1933 it was used for all classes and all worship services. The use of Danish in worship is now a distant memory, Danish ancestry is no longer as common, and Dannebrog's Lutheran Church has a declining membership; but the church remains a community church. Beth Cumming, the director of the Vacation Bible School (VBS), said that nearly every kid in the community will attend their week-long VBS program, regardless of their religious background or lack thereof.

Despite the obvious attraction of staying for the Danish beer garden and street dancing, we continued our journey. Our next destination was Farwell (pop. 148). But first, we meandered through the countryside to peak at the old Danish Lutheran Church in Nysted (St. Peder's), a Polish Catholic Church in the midst of a cornfield (Our Lady of Mount Carmel), and the Czechoslovakia cemetery just outside of Farwell. Once in Farwell we learned that the town was founded by Polish immigrants in 1887 and was originally named Posen. Arriving a few years later than their Danish neighbors, and in smaller numbers, residents decided that Posen sounded too Polish and two years later changed the name to Farwell, the Danish word for good-bye.

Even with the town's new name, the Polish heritage at St. Anthony of Padua Catholic Church is still evident. The priest at the time we visited was Father Raymond Kosmicki. The priests before him had names such as Piontkowski, Radziewicz, and Raczynski. Inside the church we picked up a pamphlet on how to make a "Traditional Polish Easter Basket." The first page listed the contents to be included and the second described the custom of "Swieconka" or the blessing of the Easter food, a tradition that was described as being "dear to the heart of every Pole." Less than ten miles to the north, the village of Elba (pop. 243), once supported a Polish newspaper and a city twenty miles to the west, Loup City (pop. 996), claims to be the Polish capital of Nebraska. If only we had arrived a week earlier, we could have attended Loup City's annual celebration of Polish Days.

Despite the heavy concentration of Poles, none of the towns was exclusively Polish or Catholic. Both Farwell and Elba once had Danish Lutheran churches, and when St.

Anthony's in Farwell was first dedicated it included forty-five families: twenty Polish, twenty Bohemian, three Irish, and two German. The fact that they reported the families by nationality signifies the importance it played in the early settlements. Considering that Elba's annual celebration is named after a Czech Bohemian pastry, "Kolache Shootout," and hosts polka bands, we concluded that several Bohemians also settled in Elba.

When we drove into the county seat of Howard County, St. Paul (pop. 2,218), the mix of ethnic congregations became even more evident. We found congregations with German Lutheran heritage, Scandinavian Lutheran ancestry, and a

A mural on the side of a building in Worms, Nebraska honors the town's ancestral connection to Worms, Germany. Along with depicting churches found in the German Worms, the painting also shows churches in the Nebraska Worms. In the upper right-hand corner of the mural is the Nebraska Worms' Zion Lutheran Church, which sits across the street from the painting (see inset picture).

Catholic congregation with multiple ethnic backgrounds. Intermingled with the old ethnic congregations were Methodists, Presbyterians, Baptists, and others.

On our return to Grand Island, we visited two small neighboring villages with strong German backgrounds. One, St. Libory, was Catholic, and the other, Worms, was Lutheran. Even though they were close to Grand Island (about twelve miles to the north), and their memberships now included commuters from the city, their German heritage was still evident. Brochures about St. Libory reported that the early pioneers arrived in 1876 and that their "ancestral home diocese was Paderborn, Westfalen, Germany." In Worms, we didn't need a brochure. Across the street from the Zion Lutheran Church, a mural painted on the side of a large building intermixed scenes from Lutheran churches in Worms, Germany, and Worms, Nebraska. Zion's pastor, Craig Niemeier, explained that the mural signified both their German heritage and their Lutheran faith.

Our brief tour of the Nebraska countryside gave us an introduction to the old immigrant congregations, but as we headed back into Grand Island we received a glimpse of the new. We stopped briefly at Cristo Cordero de Dios Lutheran Church. Formerly Trinity Lutheran and a congregation with German heritage, it now serves as a church and family center for recent Hispanic immigrants. As we journeyed back to our hotel, we continued to find more Hispanic storefronts and churches. The religious landscape was changing once again.

THE RELIGIOUS EXPERIENCE

The changing ethnic composition of central Nebraska became even more apparent when we attended a worship service at St. Mary's Catholic Church in Grand Island. St. Mary's is the cathedral for the diocese of central and western Nebraska. Like many cathedrals in America, St. Mary's is a large, majestic structure adorned with stained-glass windows, long wooden pews, and equipped with an impressive pipe organ. Two of its five Sunday Masses are now entirely in Spanish, with one at 1 p.m. and the other at 11:00 a.m., the "prime time" for Sunday worship.

We arrived before the 11:00 a.m. Mass to meet with Father Vincent Parsons, an associate pastor at St. Mary's who works closely with the Hispanic community. A native of western Nebraska, Father Parsons is not Hispanic and did not learn Spanish until after he entered the priesthood and studied in Mexico. It quickly became evident, however, that he felt close to his Hispanic members. He spoke with affection and respect about their cultures and became noticeably upset when we asked him about the Immigration and Customs Enforcement raid of a local meatpacking plant on December 12, 2006. He described the date as a "very devastating day for this community." With emotion he told of a father who took his baby to the "babysitters that morning and went to work, and because he was illegal . . . that baby stayed with that babysitter for six or seven months." The father was deported and did not see the baby again until he was able to return to the United States.

One of the two Spanish language worship services of St. Mary's Cathedral in Grand Island, Nebraska. Rosaries and other religious items are offered for sale outside the sanctuary.

At times Father Parsons would talk about the Hispanic community, but he mostly described the individual cultures and nationalities within that community, as well as noting the differences between first- and second-generation immigrants. He estimated that about 65–70 percent of the Spanish speaking members are Mexican, 20 percent are Guatemalan, and 10 percent are Salvadoran. Each group, he said, varies in how they express their religion and in the festivals they celebrate the most. For Mexicans, he noted, the Feast of Our Lady of Guadalupe is the biggest celebration of the year. He then

A prayer meeting held after the formal worship service at St. Mary's Cathedral. The meeting featured many elements common to Pentecostal worship services, such as raising of the hands and speaking in tongues.

paused and explained that the raid was conducted on the day of this celebration. "Tell me that wasn't a slap," he added.

The service we attended was similar to Roman Catholic Masses conducted everywhere. There was a confession of faith, Bible readings, prayers, a homily or short sermon, a blessing, a collection, and there was singing—much singing. The pipe organ lay silent, but the team of a dozen or so music leaders in front were armed with guitars and microphones, and they filled the church with music. Several people told us that the music team was composed almost entirely of

Guatemalans, to which they would often add, "they are very charismatic."

But if the Mass seemed lively and filled with music, it couldn't compare with the prayer meeting that followed. Sister Isabel Sandino, an immigrant from Columbia and now living in a convent in Grand Island, took us to the meeting. Held in the basement of St. Mary's educational building in a room with few decorations, the prayer meeting resembled a Pentecostal praise and worship service. Prayers were long, and members lifted their hands over their heads as they prayed, music and prayer leaders were all on an elevated stage at the front of the room, a long message was given on a Bible reading, and several participated in what Pentecostal and Charismatic Christians call "speaking in tongues." Attendance at this meeting was far less than the attendance at the morning masses. Approximately 70 people were participating, compared to the 11 a.m. attendance of 375. But the leaders stressed that it offered something that the early mass could not, and often attracted some of the most active members. Sister Sandino explained that they use many different ministries in an effort to develop more Hispanic leaders for the church and the community.

BEYOND THE CHURCH:
RELIGION IN A SMALL TOWN

Religious life in rural communities has often been seen through an idyllic and romantic filter. Rural religion conjures up Rockwellian images of entire small towns coming to a

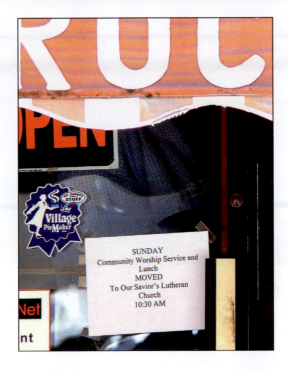

A sign on the door of a grocery store in Dannebrog, Nebraska announces a community worship service. The boundaries between "town life" and "church life" are often porous in rural communities, where the church's building and facilities often serve as the center of social and civic activity.

standstill on Sundays as men, women, and children put on their Sunday suits and dresses and head to church for a day of worship. Residents of urban areas, on the other hand, might be seen as decidedly irreligious if not outright sinful, having succumbed to the temptations of city life.

These images are not accurate now, nor were they ever accurate. In the early 1900s and probably throughout the 1800s, participation was much higher in urban areas of the U.S. Yet, as we toured central Nebraska, it became clear to us

Many religious leaders in rural communities oversee multiple, often distant, congregations. Pictured above are Pastor Gaunt and the two congregations he leads in the Ravenna area. On the bottom left is Zion Evangelical Lutheran, a small country church. Above it is Bethlehem Lutheran and its parish hall. The parish hall frequently houses many events serving the larger Ravenna community.

that the small town and countryside churches play a more extensive role in the social and civic life of their communities than is often the case for their urban counterparts. While suburbs and cities overflow with secular public spaces, social services, and community events, life in a rural community often centers on its churches.

Even as ethnicity fades in many Nebraska towns, the local churches continue to be central to their communities. Father Parsons, who has lived in several small towns in western Nebraska, said that the small town and village rely on their churches. He explained that the local church and tavern are often the final two institutions to survive in a dying town. When they're gone, he said, "you're sunk."

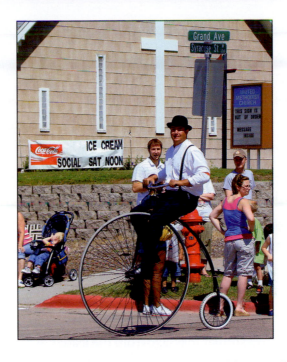

The summer festival in Ravenna, Nebraska is called Annevar (Ravenna backwards). Each year the Methodist church sponsors the festival's popular ice cream social.

Consider the town of Ravenna. About thirty miles west of Grand Island on Highway 2, Ravenna (pop. 1,341) supports four bars and four churches. The town is small but very much alive. Ravenna is one of many small towns that sprang to life when it was selected as a junction point on a railroad. The first Burlington and Missouri River train arrived in June of 1886, and Ravenna was incorporated on October 12 of that year. Today, Ravenna illustrates both the unique role of the religion in rural life and its challenges.

Father Marty Egging, the priest serving Ravenna's local Roman Catholic Church, noted that when it comes to church and community, the overlaps are many. The churches are represented in the Chamber of Commerce and have a voice in other community organizations, and the community organizations frequently use the churches' facilities. Activities that begin as church functions might later become town events or vice versa. For Father Egging, separating church and state in a small town was neither possible nor desirable. When asked about the role of rural religion within the larger context of American religion, he compared the small town church to an anchor in the sand. It slows the boat, but it doesn't stop it from moving. He went on to explain that rural churches aren't "ultra conservative," but they want to prevent "throwing out the baby with the bath water."

We heard a similar message from the leader of the Lutheran congregation in Ravenna, Pastor Micah Gaunt. Just as with Father Egging's congregation, Pastor Gaunt's parish hall is often used for community activities, such as hosting Red Cross blood drives and an occasional community fund-raiser for a family in need. As he put it, "where everybody knows everybody," the church is an essential part of social life.

One symbol of rural churches' civic role is the cemeteries so often found next to the churches. For churches located in the countryside and in tiny villages, the cemetery is an important marker of the ethnic and religious heritage of the area and serves to document a family's history. A look at the directory for the cemetery of Zion Lutheran near Hampton, Nebraska, makes it clear that it has been an important institution for many generations. The cemetery has more than 700 plots, but the surnames are frequently repeated: 20 Dobbersteins, 22 Klutes, 25 Klotzs, 29 Fensters, and so on.

None of this is to say that religion in rural communities does not present unique challenges. Sparse populations and far-flung congregations often mean that communities struggle to support their religious life. For example, many religious leaders in rural areas have to serve multiple congregations. Father Egging explained that he is now serving six congregations located in six different rural areas. Having grown up in the more sparsely populated areas of western Nebraska and having previously served three congregations covering 3,000 square miles, traveling great distances was nothing new. Serving six congregations, however, is an administrative nightmare. Father Egging lamented that he simply isn't available for all of his parishioners when they need him.

Before we left Ravenna we had the chance to capture a glimpse of the churches' involvement in the town's annual summer festival called Annevar (Ravenna spelled backwards). Once again, we missed many of the events, such as the tractor pull, the Miss Annevar and Idol contests, the pie-baking contest, and the demolition derby, but we did attend the big parade on Saturday morning. And, sure enough, the churches were involved. The Lutherans had a float in the parade, and Methodists held their popular homemade ice-cream social immediately after the parade ended. We didn't notice a float by the Catholic Church, but we did see Father Egging doing his part to build interfaith goodwill by standing in line to taste some of the Methodists' ice cream.

REFERENCES AND FURTHER READING

Carlson, Kolette. 2005. *History of Our Saviour's Lutheran Church: Dannebrog, Nebraska, 1885–2005*. Dannebrog: Our Saviour's Lutheran Church.

Mattes, Merrill J. 1969. *The Great Platte River Road: The Covered Wagon Mainline via Fort Kearny to Fort Laramie*. Lincoln: Nebraska State Historical Society.

Olson, James C., and Ronal C. Naugle. 1997. *History of Nebraska,* 3rd ed. Lincoln: University of Nebraska Press.

Shannon, James P. 1976. *Catholic Colonization on the Western Frontier*. New York: Arno Press.

Swierenga, Robert P. 1997. "The Little White Church: Religion in Rural America." *Agricultural History* 71:415–41.

University of Nebraska-Lincoln. 2010. *Virtual Nebraska: Nebraska . . . Our Towns*. http://www.casde.unl.edu/history/index.php, accessed January 2010.

Signs

As we traveled across the United States exploring its religious geography, our minds were clearly focused on the subject at hand. At times, however, we feared that weeks on the road thinking about religion had begun to play tricks on our minds, for frequently we would see signs of religion in the oddest places. And, by signs, we mean actual signs.

Congregations can be quite witty with the messages they write on their marquees. "God answers knee-mail," "This church is prayer-conditioned," and so forth. But if you look closely while exploring a place you will undoubtedly find that there are creative religious messages in much less traditional places, from highway overpasses to subway trains. These are often unsanctioned signs, or "spiritual

Someone has revised a sign in a subway car in New York City.

A sign on an antique shop in Pennsylvania provides customers an alternative destination on Sundays.

graffiti" if you will. Other times it is a store owner communicating with window shoppers.

Many of these signs were small and inconspicuous, others were hard to miss. One popular location for religious signs is along the highway, which likely says something simultaneously about the

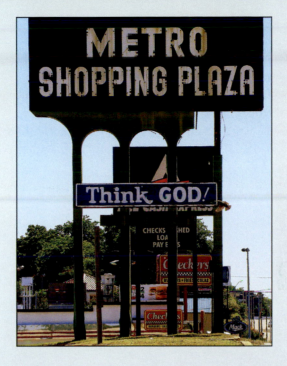

A sign at a shopping center in Memphis suggests thinking about things other than consumerism.

religious nature of the United States as well as its social and economic organization. A giant billboard in Houston, citing the Old Testament book of Chronicles, asked drivers if they had prayed for the leaders of the nation. A billboard along another highway reached out to travelers by asking, "Feeling Lost? My Book is Your Map?—God."

As the eminent social geographer Wilbur Zelinsky once wrote, "the profusion and nature of religious signs clamoring for the attention of Americans are truly extraordinary . . . these signboards function not merely to identify and inform but also to persuade the unredeemed or to reinforce the faith of believers with their brief homilies."

REFERENCES AND FURTHER READING

Fentress, Sam, and Paul Elie. 2007. *Bible Road: Signs of Faith in the American Landscape.* Cincinnati, OH: David and Charles.

Paulson, Steve, and Pam Paulson. 2009. *Church Signs Across America.* New York: Overlook Press.

York, Joe, and Charles Reagan Wilson. 2007. *With Signs Following: Photographs from the Southern Religious Roadside.* Jackson: University Press of Mississippi.

Zelinsky Wilbur. 2001. "The Uniqueness of the American Religious Landscape. *Geographical Review* 91:565–85.

SEVEN

DETROIT, MICHIGAN

Most people associate Detroit with the automobile industry. The Ford Motor Company was created in Detroit in 1903, followed by General Motors in 1908. Today, much of the industry has shifted away from the city, resulting in wrenching economic and social consequences. Still, Detroit will likely always have some claim to being the "Motor City."

Others connect Detroit with Motown Records, one of the most influential record labels in music history. Still others envision Zambonis and Stanley Cups when thinking of Detroit. The storied history of the city's professional hockey team, the Red Wings, has earned Detroit the nickname "Hockeytown USA."

What many Americans may not know, however, is that Detroit is also home to one of the largest, oldest, and most diverse Muslim populations in the United States. The Detroit area is home to an estimated fifty mosques, including the largest mosque in the United States—the Islamic Center of America.

Part of the roof of the Islamic Center of America in Dearborn, Michigan. The crescent moon has become a symbol commonly used to represent Islam. Its significance comes partly from the fact that a crescent moon marks the beginning and end of Ramadan, which is the holy month of fasting for Muslims.

THE HISTORY

People often associate Islam with the Middle East. In reality, most of the world's Muslims live outside the Middle East. Detroit reflects the incredible ethnic and cultural diversity within the Muslim population. In addition to individuals originating from places such as Lebanon, Syria, and Iraq,

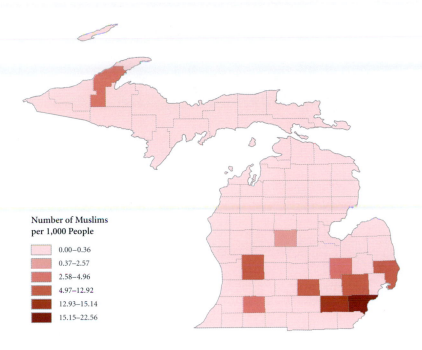

Number of Muslims
per 1,000 People

0.00–0.36
0.37–2.57
2.58–4.96
4.97–12.92
12.93–15.14
15.15–22.56

A 2000 study estimated that Michigan is home to over 80,000 Muslims. Most of these individuals reside in and around Detroit. This map shows the percentage of the county population that is estimated to be Muslim. In Wayne County, which is home to Detroit, Muslims are estimated to comprise just over 2 percent of the total population.

Detroit is home to Muslims from a wide range of other backgrounds. Some are of South Asian descent—from places such as Pakistan, Bangladesh, and India. Others are of European descent, including the countries of Albania and Bosnia.

Much of the national and ethnic diversity within Detroit's Muslim population is the result of different periods of immigration. Although some Muslims settled in Detroit in the nineteenth century, the first large wave of immigration occurred at the beginning of the twentieth century. As is often the case, there were forces both pulling Muslim immigrants to Detroit

A 1941 picture of Ford Motor Company's Rouge Plant in Dearborn, Michigan. Work on the factory began in 1917 and was completed in 1928. It attracted many immigrant workers, including many Muslims. (Library of Congress, Prints & Photographs Division, FSA/OWI Collection).

and pushing them away from their own countries. A significant Albanian Muslim population, driven by war and political strife, made Detroit its home during this time. Others, like Yemeni, Syrian, and Lebanese immigrants, came to Detroit in the early twentieth century to take advantage of economic opportunities, particularly in its burgeoning automotive sector.

Many of these immigrants went to work for the Ford Motor Co., which counted more than 550 Arabic-speaking employees in 1916. There is a legend that immigration from Yemen began after Henry Ford encountered a Yemeni sailor working on the Great Lakes. After hearing about the poverty in Yemen and its people's reputation for being hard workers—and possibly thinking that foreign workers would not unionize—Ford sent word back with the sailor that he was looking for workers and would pay five dollars for a day's work. Some said that Ford commissioned his own boat to bring workers from Yemen. Whether or not this particular story is true, to this day Ford participates in special events to recognize its continued employment of significant numbers of Muslims and the role the company has had in the Muslim history of Detroit.

The Detroit area's first mosque—a Muslim place for public prayer—was established in 1921. The opening of the mosque was accompanied by a parade, and the local newspaper, using an antiquated term for Islam, noted that "Mohammedanism had its day." Fifty years later, the majority of the city's Muslim population attended one of four congregations, each serving somewhat different populations: the Albanian Islamic Center, the American Moslem Society, Muhammad's Temple No. 1, and the Islamic Center of America.

The Albanian Islamic Center was established in 1962 and, as the name suggests, it is dominated by those of Albanian descent. The American Moslem Society, also known as the Dearborn Mosque, opened in 1937. It started by serving mainly Sunni Muslims from Lebanon who were working at a nearby Ford assembly plant. Today, the congregation's membership has diversified somewhat to include Iraqis, Yemenis, and other groups. Muhammad's Temple No. 1 was a distinctly American sect of Islam. Established by the founder of the Nation of Islam, the mosque was attended by African American Muslims and initially had few ties with other traditional

St. George Chaldean Catholic Church in Shelby Township, outside of Detroit. The Chaldean Catholic Church is an Eastern branch of the Roman Catholic Church that has an estimated 2.5 million members, most of whom reside in Iraq.

Sunni and Shia mosques. The Islamic Center of America, founded in 1963, predominantly serves Lebanese immigrants.

Waves of new immigrants arrived in Detroit in the 1960s and 1970s when the United States' immigration laws lifted restrictions on Africa, South Asian, and other non-European areas. Toward the end of the twentieth century, an additional wave occurred as Bosnian and Iraqi refugees came to the city looking to escape conflict in their own nations.

It is important to recognize that from the beginning it was not just Muslims that arrived from these nations. The Arab immigrants included a sizeable number of Christians. For example, Christians from Lebanon and Chaldean Catholics from Iraq settled in Detroit in significant numbers. Initially, some of the Christian immigrants joined existing Christian congregations, but soon Detroit was also the home to Chaldean Catholic, Syrian Orthodox, Coptic Orthodox, and other congregations worshiping in Arabic and Aramaic.

For Chaldeans, the growth was so significant that the Catholic Church now has two Chaldean and Assyrian Catholic dioceses in the United States, with six of the eight congregations in the eastern diocese located in Detroit.

THE RELIGIOUS LANDSCAPE

The number of mosques in Detroit has grown greatly in the past two decades. Some of the newer mosques are likely the product of immigration, while others are the result of splits in older mosques. As one would expect, Detroit's mosques

A makeshift storefront mosque in Detroit. Masjid As-Salam is Arabic for "Mosque of Peace."

vary greatly, from small storefront mosques to modest stand-alone congregations to large, elaborate structures.

Islam is typically said to have two main branches, Sunni and Shia, although that greatly oversimplifies its many different schools of thought. One common account dates this division to the death of its founder, Muhammad, in 632. Those who became Sunni Muslims argued that Muhammad had not designated a successor and therefore a leader should be chosen by the Muslim community. Those who became Shia Muslims argued that Muhammad had appointed his cousin as successor and that future leaders should follow the family line.

Worldwide, about 10 to 15 percent of all Muslims are said to be Shia. The percentage in Detroit is believed to be slightly higher. One study found that 18 percent of Detroit's mosques are Shia, and these tend to have a greater number of people affiliated with them than the Sunni mosques.

The size of Detroit's Muslim population has allowed it to form more ethnically concentrated mosques than are possible in many other parts of the United States. A 2004 study found about one-third of Detroit's mosques are attended largely by people of South Asian descent, while another 30 percent serve a largely Arab population. The remaining mosques are dominated by African Americans or Europeans, and a small number of mosques are attended by a fairly even mix of ethnic groups.

Despite their differences in size, ethnicity, or theology, all mosques tend to share some common features. For example, the primary function of all mosques is to serve as a place for Muslims to conduct their prayers. These prayers, or *salat*, are one of the "five pillars" that comprise the main duties of a Muslim. The primary pillar is the *shahada*, a declaration that there is a single God and that Muhammad is his prophet. The other pillars are fasting between sunrise and sunset during the month of Ramadan (*sawm*), giving to the poor (*zakat*), and making a pilgrimage to Mecca at least once in one's lifetime (*hajj*).

Within the main prayer room of a mosque there is a place in one of the walls that has an indentation or niche called a *mihrab*. This marker helps steer those praying toward the correct direction, which is facing the Saudi Arabian city of Mecca, or more specifically toward the Kaaba, a black cube-shaped building in the center of Mecca's Grand Mosque that marks the center of the Muslim world. Mecca was also the birthplace of Muhammad. Before conducting their prayers, Muslims typically go through *wudu*, a ritual cleansing of their hands, feet, and other parts of their body. As a result, most mosques have some designated area to perform this act, whether it is a separate room or part of a bathroom.

Top: The washing area at the Islamic Organization of North America in which individuals perform the ritual of ablution before conducting their prayers in the mosque. Bottom: The mihrab at the Islamic Organization of North America indicates the direction of Mecca, towards which individuals are supposed to pray.

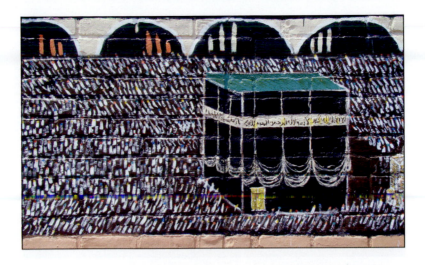

A mural on the exterior wall of the Bait-Ul-Islam Jam-E mosque in Detroit depicts individuals praying around the Kaaba in Mecca's Grand Mosque. One of the central Islamic rituals is to make pilgrimage to Mecca, called a hajj. The five-day event attracts over three million people from around the world.

Our initial overview of the landscape also revealed that relatively few of the Muslim congregations included the word "mosque" in their name. Instead, they were centers, institutes, or societies that included a mosque. The mosque was the center of activity, but their activities went well beyond the mosque.

THE RELIGIOUS EXPERIENCE

When looking to visit a mosque in Detroit, it seemed natural that we would go to the Islamic Center of America (ICA), the largest mosque in the United States. The ICA dates to 1949, when a Lebanese imam named Mohamad Jawad Chirri

The Islamic Center of America. The building covers 70,000 square feet and cost over $15 million to build. The Center attracts 800–900 people for prayers on an average Friday. On special occasions, such as the end of the fasting period called Ramadan, up to 6,000 people will enter the mosque to pray.

traveled to Detroit at the request of the local Muslim community, which was looking for a new religious leader. After some persuasion, Chirri agreed to help create and lead a new mosque. Raising the funds would take several years, and in 1959 Chirri received a $44,000 donation from Egyptian president Gamal Abdul Nasser toward the effort. What was then called the Islamic Center of Detroit finally opened in 1963.

Almost thirty years later, the congregation began planning its current building, which opened in 2005. Located on a former YMCA site, the center is across the highway from the Ford Motors corporate headquarters. In an interesting sign of Detroit and America's religious and ethnic diversity, this new building is located next to an Arabic-speaking

Lutheran Church, an Armenian Apostolic Church, a Macedonian-Bulgarian Orthodox Church, and a nondenominational Christian church. Today, the Islamic Center of America is led by the Iraqi-born imam Hassan Qazwini.

We arrived on a Thursday afternoon, the day before the primary weekly public prayer service in the mosque. Mr. Eide Alawan, the ICA's director of interfaith outreach, began by giving us a tour of the massive 122,000-square-foot facility, pointing out its bookstore, large banquet room, social and educational programs, and active youth group. He explained with enthusiasm that the ICA has played a prominent part in interfaith efforts in Detroit and the nation. He noted that Imam Qazwini has met with two U.S. presidents and gave the opening prayer for the 2003 Congress. After hearing about the many interfaith efforts he supported and seeing the size of the building, we were surprised to learn that he and most others at the center were volunteers. With little effort, he quickly listed off the few paid positions: two custodians, three part-time secretaries, one person in accounting, and two religious leaders.

Mr. Alawan ended the tour by taking us to the large circular prayer room. After taking our shoes off, we entered the room and our eyes were immediately pulled upward to the large dome, which we had seen from a distance as we approached the center. With the overhead gallery, this room has the space for more than 1,000 people to pray.

It was an impressive space. Along the walls were two bands of gold Arabic writing—verses from the Qur'an, Islam's sacred text. The floor is covered with a carpet with golden lines outlining the space where each person will sit or kneel during the gathering.

Some mosques separate men and women with a curtain during prayer. At other mosques, they pray in separate rooms. At the Islamic Center of America, women sit behind the men or in the gallery above the men's prayer area. Mr. Alawan explained that some of these traditions have varied over the years as the flow of immigrants has changed.

Echoing the stories we heard from other mosques and Christian congregations in the area, he noted that the recent immigrants want a more traditional religion and more traditional family roles. For example, in the early 1970s, the Islamic Center hosted wedding dances. At that time Imam Chirri was clean-shaven and often wore Western-style suits. But the dances ended and Imam Chirri's beard and traditional dress returned when a new wave of immigrants came from Iran in the late 1970s.

We arrived early at the mosque on Friday to attend the main prayer gathering. Once inside, we watched as individuals performed the prayer ritual called *raka'ah*, which involves reciting verses from the Qur'an, bowing with hands on knees, then leaning forward with the hands and head on the ground, and finally sitting back with the feet under the body. After completing the *raka'ah*, many people sat quietly and read the Qur'an. As the mosque filled, there was also a public reading of the Qur'an. Although there were no chairs, many of the older men sat at the edge of the room where they could lean against the wall.

As the mosque continued to fill, a man called the *muezzin* came to the podium to announce that the group (juma)

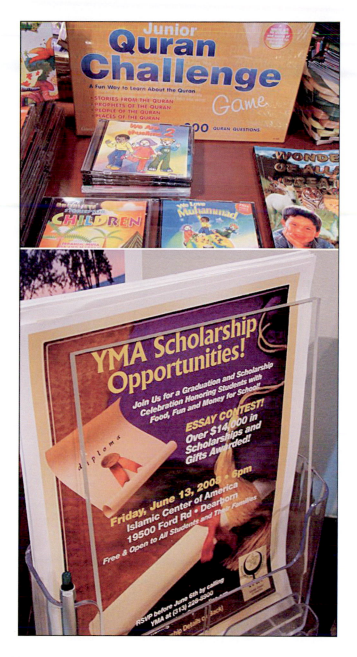

Top: Religious education resources for youth in the bookstore at the Islamic Center of America. Bottom: Fliers at the Islamic Center of America advertise an event organized by the mosque's youth group celebrating the high school graduation of some of its members and a contest to win college scholarships.

Scenes from inside the Islamic Center of America's mosque during Friday prayers.

prayer was about to begin. Then Imam Qazwini came to the
podium to lead the prayer and deliver a message or sermon.
He spoke first in Arabic, then in English. Some portions of
the message were distinctively Islamic. Other portions
sounded similar to messages we had heard at other houses of
worship in previous weeks. Like Pastor Cole in Memphis and

the elders at the Mormon ward, Imam Qazwini told parents that they must give their children guidance during the summer months, and reminded them of the center's events and activities for children. Like the Christian congregations we visited, the Islamic Center of America wanted to have an impact that went far beyond the weekly prayer gathering.

BEYOND THE MOSQUE

As we toured mosques in the Detroit area we found that each of them was typically accompanied with an array of other facilities, such as kitchens, libraries, schools, media centers, and social halls. This may not seem like something worth pointing out, since many Christian and Jewish congregations also offer much more than a room for a weekly worship service. But this is a pattern that is somewhat unique, at least when compared to mosques in nations that are predominantly Muslim.

Muslim leaders were quick to acknowledge these differences from their "old countries." When asked to explain, Imam Elturk of Islamic Organizations of North America offered this succinct, yet powerful, explanation: "[i]n the old countries we were living in an Islamic culture, here we must create one." He then went on to add that they "create a culture through social events, and that requires a kitchen, food . . ." and then he waved his hands as if to signify "and so on." Mr. Alawan of the Islamic Center of America offered a similar assessment. He pointed out that the multidimensional nature of many U.S. mosques is hinted at in their names, "we call this the Islamic Center. And it's a center . . . it has other things happening. The mosque is this area, and the other end of it is the center." He went on to explain that many of the services and opportunities that Islamic centers provide in the United States can be found in the larger community in countries with a large Muslim population.

Even though the facilities of the Islamic Center of America are larger and more elaborate than most of the Islamic

An Islamic clothing store on Warren Avenue.

centers we toured, the "extracurricular" features and services were often very similar. Whereas the ICA had a social hall that could seat 1,200 people for dinner and 2,500 for a lecture, nearly all of the centers had some similar room. Few, if any, could match the size of the Islamic Center of America's bookstore, but they all had books and brochures available for visitors, and a library was prominent in many mosques. Without exception, all of the Muslim congregations we visited had activities for children and youth. From summer camps to Arabic classes to sporting and social activities, this mosque offered activities and groups that were distinctively Muslim. Mr. Alawan explained that the "fear is that you're going to lose your children to another faith" because they are living "in a sea of a Christian country."

A few of the centers have also established private religious schools, much in the same way Catholic, Lutheran, and Jewish adherents in the United States have done. The first such high school, the American Islamic Academy, was created by a mosque called the Islamic Institute of Knowledge. The school later became a public charter school called the Riverside Academy–West. Although it is not formally a religious school, it still maintains some of its original character, student population, and informal ties to the mosque next door. The Islamic Center of America started the Muslim American Youth Academy in 1998. This school now enrolls 365 students from preschool to eighth grade. Like other parochial schools, the school supplements the standard Michigan curriculum with religious instruction and includes prayer in the schedule. For Muslim schools the additional instruction often includes studies in Arabic, Islam, and the Qur'an.

In addition to forming places for prayer and "centers" near their mosques, Muslim immigrants and their descendants have established many businesses and community organizations to help continue their traditions and culture in their new home. Some are distinctly Muslim; others are shared with all immigrants from similar cultures. Today, for example, a person driving down Warren Avenue or through some of the other ethnic enclaves will find restaurants serving cuisine in the style of their nations of origin. Organizations, such as the Arab Community Center for Economic and Social Services, are "committed to the development of the Arab American community," regardless of religion.

You will also find businesses and organizations catering to the unique religious needs of Detroit's Muslim population.

Many small ethnic grocery stores advertise *halal* food, a term that describes food that meets Islamic dietary restrictions and standards. Given the size of Detroit's Muslim population, more mainstream stores have tried to cater to these needs as well. A 2000 *Detroit Free Press* article noted that a local McDonald's had begun to sell "halal McNuggets," while several other chain stores in Detroit were also beginning to offer similar products. You will also find stores offering clothing that meets the religious standards of adherents, such as the head covering, or *hijab*, worn by some Muslim women.

The September 11, 2001 terrorist attacks were a defining moment for Detroit's Muslim community. In the wake of the attacks some non-Muslim Americans looked, often with an accusatory eye, at the entire Muslim population. This tension was felt acutely among Detroit's Muslims. When the Islamic Organization of North America, a largely Pakistani mosque, tried to establish itself in a Detroit suburb, it faced a great deal of resistance from some in the community. Some people expressed concerns about noise or traffic, but other concerns were clearly based on misconceptions or prejudices against Muslims.

At the same time, though, many local religious leaders from a wide variety of faiths spoke in defense of the mosque. Indeed, despite the occasional negative incident or statement, most people in Detroit saw the attacks as an opportunity to learn more about their Muslim neighbors, and many of the area mosques were more than happy to discuss their faith with visitors. As Imam Elturk of the Islamic Organization of North America told us, "This curiosity all of a sudden became so open and people just wanted to know more about Islam. So that gave us a chance to present ourselves to the larger community."

REFERENCES AND FURTHER READING

Abraham, Nabeel, and Andrew Shryock. 2000. *Arab Detroit: From Margin to Mainstream*. Detroit: Wayne State University Press.

Alawan, Raad I. 2005. "New Beginnings: The Story of the Islamic Center of America." In the *Islamic Center of America Grand Opening Commemorative Journal*, 27–38.

Bagby, Ihsan. 2004. *A Portrait of Detroit Mosques: Muslim Views on Policy, Politics and Religion*. Clinton Township, MI: Institute for Social Policy and Understanding.

Curtis, Edward E. IV. 2009. *Muslims in America: A Short History*. New York: Oxford University Press.

Dunbar, Willis F., and George S. May. 1995. *Michigan: A History of the Wolverine State*. Grand Rapids, MI: William B. Eerdmans.

Esposito, John L. 2006. "Islam." *World Encyclopedia of Religious Practices*. Detroit: Gale.

Haddad, Yvonne Yazbeck, and Jane I. Smith. 2002. *Muslim Minorities in the West: Visible and Invisible*. Walnut Creek, CA: Altamira Press.

Hassoun, Rosina J. 2005. *Arab Americans in Michigan*. East Lansing: Michigan State University Press.

Public Broadcasting Service. *Islam: Empire of Faith*. Film and educational resources available at http://www.pbs.org/empires/islam/index.html

Howell, Sally, and Andrew Shryock. 2008. Building Islam in Detroit: Foundation, Forms, Futures. An Exhibit Sponsored by the University of Michigan. See http://www.umich.edu/~biid/index.html

Monastery of the Transfiguration

WELL OFF THE BEATEN PATH and nestled in the wooded hills of rural Pennsylvania, we heard about a small monastery established by a Romanian princess. We could not resist learning more. Founded in 1967 as the first English-speaking Orthodox monastery in the United States, the Monastery of the Transfiguration is in a quiet and secluded setting: a well-hidden spot on the American religious landscape. We quickly learned, however, that even though the facilities are modest and the location is remote, the story of this monastery and its founder, Mother Alexandra, is quite exceptional.

Mother Alexandra was born on January 5, 1909, but at that time she was known as Princess Ileana, the daughter of King Ferdinand and Queen Maria of Romania. Ileana came from a long line of royalty: her mother was the granddaughter of Queen Victoria of Britain and the tsar of Russia, Alexander II. The princess married Archduke Anton of Austria, raised six children, and established a hospital for wounded Romanian soldiers during World War II. Despite her illustrious roots, much of her early life was consumed with Romania's tumultuous politics and with family turmoil.

Princess Ileana eventually sought peace in the monastic life, taking her first vows as a monastic in France in 1965. Two years later she took her final vows and became Mother Alexandra. She then went to the United States to start the Orthodox Monastery of the Transfiguration. Her goal was to have an English-speaking convent where women of all ethnic backgrounds could come together. She served

Hidden in a wooded area of rural Pennsylvania, the Orthodox Monastery of the Transfiguration has a unique history that includes a connection to European royalty.

as the first abbess, but later stepped aside. This allowed a fellow Romanian, Mother Benedicta, to lead the monastery. More experienced in the monastic life, Mother Benedicta instituted the full "cycle of prayers" used in other Orthodox monasteries.

Sister Vicki, a nun at the monastery, gave us and other guests an introduction to the chapel and life at the monastery today. She explained

On the left, the monastery's nuns meet around a table for dinner. On the right, a nun shows us around the monastery's chapel.

that unlike cloistered monasteries, the sisters at the Monastery of the Transfiguration welcome guests, devoting their lives to hospitality and prayer. As a result, the monastery serves as a spiritual retreat center for many people and as a monastic home for nine sisters. The highlight of the chapel tour for Sister Vicki was explaining the chapel icons. The guests loved this, too. With both patience and excitement, Sister Vicki told the story of each icon and answered a litany of questions.

When the tour was over, we sat in the library where she invited still more questions and spoke openly about monastic life. She acknowledged the many joys and challenges of communal living. She reviewed the daily schedule of joining others for early morning prayers, late afternoon prayers, and the physical work that fell between. Before coming to a monastery she explained that she longed to have more time for prayer. She still treasures her time in prayer, but she said that she now realizes that extended prayer requires focus, concentration, and surrender. In short, prayer can be hard work.

REFERENCES AND FURTHER READING

Cooke, Bev. 2008. *Royal Monastic: Princess Ileana of Romania*. Ben Lomond, CA: Conciliar Press Ministries.

BROOKLYN, NEW YORK

A s we emerged from the Holland Tunnel onto the streets of Manhattan, we knew we were in "the city." Masses of people swarmed between buildings. Everywhere we turned, the city seemed to serve as a testament to the ingenuity and technological prowess of modern humans. Even the street names are synonymous with centers of American secular life, from Wall Street, a financial center, to Broadway, a cultural mecca. But rarely do these sights conjure up feelings of the sacred. Once engulfed in this sea of modern culture, technology, and humanity it seemed apt to ask: Is there anywhere more "worldly" than New York City?

Yet, as we crossed the East River into Brooklyn, we were greeted by a paradox, for here there are communities living a lifestyle that seems to challenge the urban, modern environment in which they exist. Hasidic Jews have established entire neighborhoods within the city that allow them to live apart

A Hasidic man and his children walk on the streets of New York City.

from a surrounding culture that seems to threaten many of their beliefs and practices. We came here to explore this paradox. And while Brooklyn's Hasidic communities may be the most visible, they are only one piece of the larger story of Jews in New York City and in America.

THE HISTORY

Although there is evidence that a handful of Jews set foot in the colonies earlier, most historical accounts begin in 1654. In that year, twenty-three Jewish refugees arrived from Brazil in the Dutch settlement of New Amsterdam, which would later become New York City. This group had fled Brazil after Portugal took the land from the Dutch and forced out the Protestant and Jewish residents. By the end of the seventeenth century, a Jewish congregation was established in New York.

The Jewish community in the United States remained small—an estimated 2,000 people at the time of the American Revolution. This would not change significantly until the

A view of the Brooklyn Bridge looking south from Manhattan toward Brooklyn Heights. (Library of Congress, Prints and Photographs Division, Historic American Engineering Record.)

1840s, when large numbers of Jews from Germany and other central European nations arrived seeking economic opportunity and freedom from persecution. The Jewish population grew quickly, from approximately 5,000 in 1830 to roughly 150,000 by 1860.

A second wave of Jewish immigrants—an estimated 2 million of them—arrived between 1880 and 1914, primarily from eastern Europe. They brought with them distinctive ethnic, cultural, economic, and religious traditions. The established Jewish communities had assimilated into American life and culture. Their religious practices did not make them stand out in society in any way, as they had compartmentalized their faith into occasional attendance at a synagogue's worship service. The service was given in English in a style similar to that of many Protestant churches. However, these new Jewish immigrants brought a much more traditional and religiously saturated lifestyle to the United States. They established Jewish enclaves that included not only synagogues but also a wide variety of stores, associations, and organizations to serve their religious needs.

The contrasts between the established Jewish population and these new eastern European Jewish immigrants would eventually produce a formal organizational and theological divide that remains today. On the one side were the more modernist, Americanized, "Reform" Jews who would establish the Union of American Hebrew Congregations along with the Hebrew Union College to train its rabbis. On the other side were the more traditional, "Orthodox" Jews that would eventually establish the Orthodox

Jewish Congregational Union of America and the Jewish Theological Seminary.

The split between these groups was dramatically fore-shadowed in 1883 at a dinner held to celebrate the ordination of the Hebrew Union College's first cohort of rabbis. The meal included several items that violated the traditional Jewish dietary rules. Guests who adhered to more orthodox beliefs and practices were angered and offended. The experience motivated them to create their own organization and institutions to honor their dietary practices and other traditions. This incident is referred to the as the "trefa," or nonkosher, banquet.

Today, Jews are typically organized into three major groups: Orthodox, Conservative, and Reform. The Conservative movement attempts to preserve some of the traditions of the Orthodox branch while also instituting some of the Reform branch's nods to modern American society. When you look closer, however, multiple schisms appear. Nowhere is this more evident than among Orthodox Jews, where divisions occur within the divisions.

One of the more noticeable branches of Orthodox Judaism is the Hasidim. Hasidic Jews came to the United States primarily after World War II, in the wake of the destruction that the war and the Holocaust had imposed on their European communities. The tradition began, though, in the early eighteenth century with the teachings of Rabbi Israel ben Eliezer, who is better known as the Baal Shem Tov. The Baal Shem Tov, or "Master of the Good Name," is said to have performed miracles in the Ukraine. After his death, his disciples continued to spread his teachings in Europe.

Hasidic Jews are in some ways similar to other Orthodox Jews, but they also have a unique history and distinct beliefs and practices. Hasidic Judaism emphasizes pietism, or an intense devotion to religious practice and the laws of the Jewish faith. "Hasidism" actually means "pious ones." Not surprisingly, they are sometimes referred to as "ultra-Orthodox."

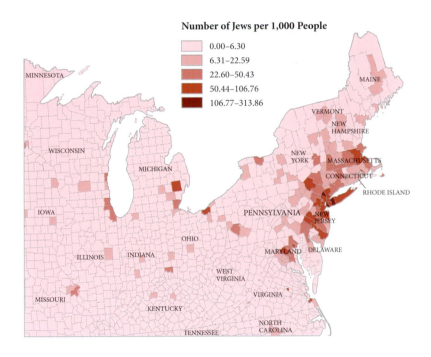

Number of Jews per 1,000 People

- 0.00–6.30
- 6.31–22.59
- 22.60–50.43
- 50.44–106.76
- 106.77–313.86

A map of the estimated percentage of the population (by county) that is Jewish. Although there are significant populations on the West coast and in Florida, New York City has been historically and remains to this day the center of the American Jewish community. (Source: Religious Congregations and Membership Study; The Association of Religion Data Archives, www.theARDA.com.)

Hasidism also contains a stronger mystical tradition, which emphasizes individuals' ability to experience or become one with God, than does standard Orthodox Judaism.

It is not accurate to speak of a single Hasidic community or a single Hasidic tradition. There are roughly two dozen Hasidic groups, each the result of some schism or conflict within the larger history and practice of Hasidism. Some of the major groups include the Satmar, the Chabad-Lubavitch, and the Bobov. Each of these individual communities is loyal to a particular rebbe, or spiritual leader.

The position of the rebbe is frequently passed down from father to son. Rebbes are seen as extraordinary individuals with powers that go far beyond those of a regular rabbi. They also, on occasion, take on even greater significance. Although there are different interpretations of the meaning and nature of the "messiah," Orthodox Jews, including Hasidic Jews, hold a belief that eventually one will come. Occasionally a rebbe has been labeled by their followers as a potential messiah. This was most recently the case in the Chabad-Lubavitch community. Rabbi Menachem Mendel Schneerson, who served as the seventh Lubavitcher rebbe, died in 1994. In the years leading up to his death and to this day, some in the Lubavitch community believed that Schneerson was the Messiah. Pictures of Schneerson remain plastered around Lubavitch neighborhoods in Brooklyn—a testament to the importance and admiration of the community for the rebbe.

The differences between the various Hasidic communities go beyond their respective leaders. Each group has its own unique views, traditions, and practices. In fact, some of the

A Hasidic man visits a Hebrew magazine stand on the streets of Brooklyn. Hasidic Jews, particularly men, are known for their distinctive dress and appearance.

communities hold hostile feelings toward each other. For example, the Chabad-Lubavitch community is well known for its efforts to proselytize nonpracticing Jews and even win over members from other Hasidic communities. This has raised the ire of other communities, particularly the Satmar. At times, the tension between these communities has boiled over into violence.

The New York City area has always been the center of American Jewish life, regardless of ethnic, cultural, or theological differences, from the original Brazilian refugees who landed in New Amsterdam to the Hasidic Jews who arrived after World War II.

THE RELIGIOUS LANDSCAPE

In 2000 an estimated 1,000 Jewish congregations existed in the state of New York—twice as many as California, the state with the second highest number. More than 250 are located in Brooklyn.

We began our tour at the Brooklyn Heights Synagogue, where we spoke at length with Rabbi Serge Lippe. A Reform synagogue, it was established in 1960 to serve local residents who were tired of traveling long distances to attend services. Even though Reform Jews, unlike the Orthodox, are allowed

Rabbi Serge Lippe of the Reform Brooklyn Heights Synagogue.

to drive and ride public transportation on the Sabbath, Rabbi Lippe noted that 70 percent of his synagogue's members live within walking distance. He described his congregation and the larger neighborhood as an "urban village."

As is the case with most Reform congregations, Rabbi Lippe's synagogue is lenient when it comes to many traditional Jewish laws concerning dress, diet, and other behaviors. For example, as we were about to enter the worship space we walked past prayer shawls and yarmulkes (skull caps). The rabbi explained that no one was required to wear these unless he or she was comfortable doing so. Rabbi Lippe stressed that Reform Jews are inclusive and egalitarian. For example, Reform Jews do not follow the Orthodox tradition of separate seating areas for women and men during worship.

This leniency or progressiveness contrasted sharply with what we saw and heard at the Congregation B'nai Avraham, an Orthodox synagogue located a block away in a building once used by the Brooklyn Heights Synagogue. Led by Rabbi Aaron Raskin, who is part of the Hasidic Chabad-Lubavitch group, Congregation B'nai Avraham is generally regarded as a "modern Orthodox" community. This means that many of the members do not adhere as strictly to the rules and are not as withdrawn as members of most Hasidic communities. Yet, their worship and daily practices are far more traditional in content and style than those found at a Reform synagogue. For example, the seating at the congregation is gender-segregated, with women in the rear of the sanctuary separated from the men by a room divider.

Congregation B'nai Avraham was started when a couple who had been attending a Conservative synagogue wanted a more observant shul (congregation). They turned to the Chabad-Lubavitch headquarters because they were known for providing rabbis, even when a congregation had only a few members. One of the members noted that "when young Rabbi Raskin came to the group he had no beard, no wife, and no children." Twenty years later "he now has a beard, a wife, six children and the congregation has grown exponentially."

Rabbi Raskin is a charismatic man who takes a great deal of pride in speaking with others about his congregation and his faith. With enthusiasm, he introduced us to individuals who passed through the synagogue and encouraged us to speak with them about their experiences. He also gave us a tour of what was one of his proudest achievements—the ritual bath or mikvah located in the synagogue's basement.

Rabbi Raskin said that, according to Jewish law, women are considered impure while they are menstruating and for a few days afterwards. During this time their husbands should not have physical contact with them. When this period is over, they immerse themselves in the ritual bath, and the couple can resume contact. Rabbi Raskin argued that even if a person did not subscribe to the beliefs underlying the mikvah, it was a great way to maintain a happy marriage, because after twelve days of having no contact the couple's relationship will be "explosive."

After leaving Rabbi Raskin's congregation, we decided to move even farther along the continuum of American Judaism and spend some time visiting Brooklyn's Hasidic

Rabbi Raskin of the Orthodox Congregation B'nai Avraham. Although Rabbi Raskin and Rabbi Lippe of the Brooklyn Heights Synagogue represent two different strains of American Judaism, the two leaders work closely together in their neighborhood.

neighborhoods, of which there are several, including Borough Park and Crown Heights. In the latter you will find the world headquarters of the Chabad-Lubavitch group. Located at 770 Eastern Parkway, the Chabad community refers to it simply as "770."

The building was acquired in 1940 and served as the office and residence of the sixth Lubavitcher rebbe who, having escaped Nazi Germany, died in 1950. In addition to serving as

The headquarters of the Chabad-Lubavitch Hasidic community in Brooklyn is a place bustling with activity as men gather to pray at all times during the day. Many of the men pictured are wearing a prayer shawl and tefillin. Tefillin consist of leather straps around the body and head with small square boxes that contains parchment with Torah verses written on them.

the administrative headquarters of the Chabad movement, 770 also serves as a place of prayer and worship. When we stopped by, more than one hundred men were gathered for prayer. As we walked around the room, several people stopped to speak about their faith and practices. Members repeatedly told us that they don't just go through the motions during rituals. Rather, they understood them and said they were critical avenues of spiritual growth. They also expressed their ongoing admiration and affection for the late Rebbe Schneerson, who died in 1994, and of his significance to "770." One man showed us the corner of the room where the rebbe used to speak.

There are a number of other noteworthy Hasidic sites in Brooklyn. In the Borough Park neighborhood, for example, Congregation Shomrei Shabbos offers around-the-clock prayer. Orthodox Jewish law states that a minyan, or gathering of ten adult men, is required in order to hold communal prayers. While most congregations only offer such prayers at certain times, at the Shomrei Shabbos synagogue enough men can be found at any time of the day to hold prayers. Businesses around the synagogue stay open late or all night to cater to the crowds that gather to pray, whether it is 2:00 p.m. or 2:00 a.m.

THE RELIGIOUS EXPERIENCE

Our visits to the synagogues and sites of Brooklyn allowed us to observe the communal prayers, tour the worship areas and visit the larger Jewish community. Now we were ready to experience the Sabbath. Although we had been warmly invited to join several congregations for their Saturday morning service, we decided to attend the service of Rabbi Raskin's Orthodox Congregation, B'nai Avraham.

The Jewish Shabbat, or Sabbath, begins at sundown on Friday and ends Saturday evening. What this means for an individual varies depending on the branch of Judaism to which he adheres. For Reform Jews, Shabbat may be similar to any other day of the week, though Friday night worship is popular at many synagogues. Conservative Jews typically refrain from many forms of "work" activities, but specific forbidden activities vary by synagogue. For Orthodox Jews, however, Shabbat involves a long list of restrictions. They don't drive, carry objects, or engage in activities that might be considered "work" under rabbinical law. Being an Orthodox congregation with a Hasidic rabbi, B'nai Avraham attendees lean toward this more stringent interpretation of Shabbat. At least one of the attendees walked an hour to get to the synagogue wearing a traditional long black coat on a very hot and humid July day. Using a car or subway would have been a violation of Shabbat rules.

When we entered the synagogue, a large Israeli flag was draped above the hallway. Two doors on the right led to the sanctuary (worship area). The first door opened to the women's seating area and the second to the men's. Seeing that we were visitors, two young boys came to offer advice. They instructed us to leave our cell phones in the hall (though one admitted they might play with them), told us which door to enter, and made sure our heads were covered with yarmulkes. Upon entering the worship space, we saw a platform (bimah) in the center of the room. There, several men were taking turns reading Hebrew prayers aloud. All of the men were wearing prayer shawls and yarmulkes. Most wore modern dress but a few had the long beards and clothing associated with Hasidic Jews. Behind the podium was the women's seating area, blocked from view by room dividers. Several sets of pews were beside and in front of the podium, and at the front of the room was a slightly raised area on which sat the ark, the sacred cabinet-like structure that contains the handwritten Torah scrolls. The Torah, the first five books of the Hebrew Bible, is the part of Scripture that outlines Jewish law.

After we took our seats, a couple of men welcomed us and helped to orient us during the service. Although the service was in Hebrew, the readers assisted us by announcing in English the page numbers of the readings, which allowed us to follow the English translation. The prayers included specific requests for Israel, the United States, and for the health and well-being of Jews and non-Jews. We would later learn that several of those attending were from Israel, and there were immigrants from Russia, Israel, France, Peru, Iran, and Yemen as well.

The climax of the service came when the Torah scroll was removed from the ark for a reading. Everyone rose to their feet as the scroll was carried around the room, including the women's seating area. As the scroll passed, people touched its cover using a corner of their prayer shawls, a sign of reverence and affection for the Torah.

After the prayers and readings, Rabbi Simcha Weinstein gave a brief talk. Prior to becoming a rabbi he had a career in filmmaking. He knew how to engage an audience. He asked the congregation if it was necessary to follow all of the 613 mitzvot or commandments. In particular, he focused on the restrictions of the Sabbath, such as not driving or riding in a car. He argued that while it may seem to make sense that one simply drive to the synagogue on a very hot day, such violations of the rules have unintended consequences. For example, if a person can drive to the synagogue then they do not need to live near the synagogue. If they do not need to live near the synagogue, then the entire community of the congregation suffers.

At the conclusion of the service, we were invited to join the congregation's reception or kiddush. As we entered the reception area we saw a table filled with food, including crackers and herring. Before we could get to the food, however, several men encouraged us to join them in a toast. Pouring small glasses of vodka they explained that it was traditional to say "*l'chaim*," or "to life," before partaking. So, we toasted to life—a few times, maybe more.

BEYOND THE SYNAGOGUE

Strong, close-knit communities are typically associated with small-town America, where the biggest weekly event in some towns is Friday's high school football game. New York City, on the other hand, is seldom seen as a place that cultivates "community" because of its massive population. But we found that in parts of Brooklyn having masses of people crammed in a relatively small space can lead to a strong sense of community.

Rabbi Lippe lives five minutes away from his Reform Brooklyn Heights Synagogue. Yet, he told us, it takes him at least half an hour to get home each day because as he walks, he constantly stops to speak with people he knows in the neighborhood. Despite the extreme urban setting of New York City, or perhaps because of it, Jews have found ways to build and rebuild their communities beyond the synagogue.

Rabbi Weinstein explained that the density of the population is what makes a strong Jewish community possible. Orthodox Jews can walk to synagogue, and all Jews can be close to kosher markets, Hebrew schools, and other institutions that are distinctively Jewish.

Nowhere is this more apparent than in the Hasidic neighborhood of Borough Park. As we walked through the neighborhood there was little doubt about the population that resides, shops, and worships there. The dress of the pedestrians was the first and most obvious sign that we had entered a Hasidic neighborhood. We soon found blocks upon blocks of businesses, schools, and agencies devoted to maintaining the Hasidic lifestyle and community. Kosher restaurants and grocery stores offer food that adheres to Jewish standards, and the local newsstands had multiple Hebrew publications. The dozens of maternity stores reflect the very high fertility rate of Hasidic families. Wig stores serve Jewish women whose hair must be covered in accordance with Jewish law. Many of the other neighborhood shops sold music, books, clothing, cosmetics, toys, crafts, and gifts that catered to the Jewish residents. We even found a Kosher Day Spa.

Along with providing a seemingly endless selection of distinctively Jewish goods, the Hasidic communities and

A wide variety of stores and services support the devout lifestyle of Orthodox and Hasidic Jews in Brooklyn. These range from stores with prayer supplies to ambulance and school bus services dedicated to the Jewish population.

the larger Brooklyn Jewish community also provide a vast array of Jewish services. The yeshiva schools that train boys and girls in Jewish theology and traditions are the most ubiquitous examples. When we returned to our hotel that evening we found well over one hundred yeshivas listed in the Brooklyn Yellow Pages. Plus, there are many distinctively Jewish service agencies scattered across Brooklyn, such the Jewish Board of Family and Children's Services, the Jewish Association for Services for the Aged, Jewish Community Centers, and the Meir Panim, an agency supporting relief societies in Israel. We also saw numerous posters and flyers advertising camps for Jewish children and concerts of Jewish music. One particularly interesting example of a distinctively Jewish service is Hatzolah, an ambulance service. Because Orthodox and especially Hasidic Jews have many concerns about contact between men and women as well as many other religious and cultural beliefs that may make secular ambulance services undesirable, they have formed their own volunteer ambulance services, or Hatzolahs, to alleviate these concerns.

The ability of Hasidic Jews to form such communities in New York City is amazing, especially given the relatively short period of time in which it has been accomplished. But it is not without complications and costs. The high fertility rate of the Hasidic families creates an ever-growing population in need of housing in a city where there is little room to spread out. Partly due to these dynamics, the Hasidic communities have clashed with other ethnic groups and even non-Hasidic Jews over control of neighborhoods. Their devotion to an intense religious lifestyle has produced economic problems as their restricted levels of education and desire to remain within their enclaves often severely limits their opportunities. Poverty is common in Hasidic communities.

Despite these many challenges, we found a vibrant, tight-knit community that was clearly organized around Judaic laws and teachings. When we returned to Borough Park on a Friday afternoon, the distinctiveness of the community became even more obvious. By mid-afternoon, with Shabbat arriving in a few hours, shops were closing and traffic gradually disappeared. Even Eichlers, the Judaic superstore, closed several hours before Shabbat began. In Borough Park and in other Hasidic neighborhoods across Brooklyn, "the city" gave way to the "urban village" on Shabbat.

REFERENCES AND FURTHER READING

Buber, Martin. 1960. *The Origin and Meaning of Hasidism*. Edited and translated by Maurice Friedman. New York: Harper and Row.

Garvin, Philip, and Arthur A. Cohen. 1970. *A People Apart: Hasidism in America*. New York: E. P. Dutton and Co, Inc.

Lando, Michal. January 28, 2007. "In the Wee Hours, Worship and More." *New York Times*.

Mintz, Jerome R. 1992. *Hasidic People: A Place in the New World*. Cambridge, MA: Harvard University Press.

Marcus, Jacob Rader. 1995. *The American Jew, 1585–1990: A History*. Brooklyn. NY: Carlson Publishing Inc.

Raphael, Marc Lee. 2003. *Judaism in America*. New York: Columbia University Press.

Sarna, Jonathan D. 2004. *American Judaism: A History*. New Haven, CT: Yale University Press.

Sexton, Joe. April 21, 1997. "When Work is Not Enough: Religion and Welfare Shape Economics for the Hasidim." *New York Times*.

A group of young Amish men and women return home from Sunday worship. Amish men are clean-shaven prior to marriage, but a beard is required after they are married.

The Amish

THE AMISH LIFESTYLE SEEMS so different from what most of us experience. Watching an Amish farmer direct a team of horses or seeing an Amish family drive into town with their horse and buggy only reinforces this impression. When combined with their distinctive wardrobes, unique hairstyles, and small rural schools that end at eighth grade, the chasm between Amish and others seems wide and undeniable. For some, these differences seem quaint, for others they are just plain strange. As we interacted with the Amish of central Pennsylvania, however, we quickly learned that these differences are not as great as they first seem.

When you first talk with the Amish you need to remind yourself not to stare at their appearance or ask dumb questions. Do they use

An Amish farmer utilizes a team of horses in lieu of a tractor.

zippers? Are those clothes really comfortable? Eventually, however, you begin to listen to their stories and find they are very similar to your own. For example, just as the "English" (non-Amish) agonize over how much freedom to give their teenagers or how to deal with an aging parent, so do the Amish. One Amish family shared with us their concerns about their aging grandfather. The family wanted him to have the independence of driving his own horse and buggy. Yet, time after time he would forget how to get home. The decision point came when he turned in front of a car passing his buggy, and his horse was killed. Like the painful decision of taking away an aging parent or grandparent's car, they decided it was time for grandpa to stop driving his buggy. Grandpa does not remember the accident, and he sure doesn't understand why they took his horse away.

Just as we fail to notice the similarities between us and them, we often fail to notice the differences between the various Amish communities. The Old Order Amish is the largest group, but they are one of many. Like all other religious groups, the Amish have splintered into many different sects. In neighboring Mifflin County the various groups include Byler Amish, Peachy Amish, Nebraska Amish, Zook Amish, and several different Mennonite groups. Some are far more rigid than the Old Order Amish, and others are far more lenient. The most noticeable differences between the groups are their use of technology and, for some, the clothing they wear or the types of buggies they drive. The Byler Amish, for example, are the only sect to drive yellow-top buggies.

Perhaps the most important differences, and the source of many schisms, are how they define community and the practice of shunning (*Meidung*) those who fail to follow the community rules (*Ordnung*). As the Amish generally worship in each other's homes, the local districts or congregations are organized geographically, allowing all families to have a short buggy ride to attend worship. As a result, the local congregation is at the heart of Amish life; and determining the rules, including how membership is defined, is of great importance to the community. Although each congregation identifies with one of the "orders," there is substantial variation from one district or congregation to the next.

We still cannot hitch a horse to a buggy, but as we interacted with the Amish the chasm of differences between us began to close. At the same time, the diversity within the "them" began to appear.

REFERENCES AND FURTHER READING

Hostetler, John A. 1963. *Amish Society*. Baltimore, MD: The John Hopkins University Press.

Kraybill, Donald B. 2001. *The Riddle of Amish Culture*. Baltimore, MD: The John Hopkins University Press.

Kreps, George M., Joseph F. Donnermeyer, and Marty W. Kreps. 2004. *A Quiet Moment in Time: A Contemporary View of Amish Society*. Sugarcreek, OH: Carlisle Printing.

Schaefer, Richard T., and William W. Zellner. 2008 *Extraordinary Groups: An Examination of Unconventional Lifestyles*. New York: Worth Publishers.

RETURNING HOME: CENTRAL PENNSYLVANIA

W e began our tour by systematically selecting locations that we knew were unique and important parts
of America's religious geography. Even though we knew quite
a bit about the places and groups we visited before embark-
ing on this journey, we were often impressed and amazed by
what we observed. Yet, perhaps the greatest lessons came
from the places we did not plan on visiting. The stops between
the scheduled destinations, whether an overnight stay or a
lunch taken in the middle of a long drive, taught us that every
place, regardless of size or region, has an interesting story.
Not every community can claim to have the largest mosque
in the United States or a church that seats 16,000. Still, as we
went from state to state and drove through hundreds of
towns we found that every community is its own unique
place of faith.

A sign in the village of Gatesburg, Pennsylvania announces the small community's 200th anniversary. Across the street is the Gatesburg Lutheran Church, whose sign reads "Thank You God for Gatesburg."

We close this tour by returning to the communities of central Pennsylvania, which is our home. We did not originally identify our own backyard as being a significant part of America's religious history or geography, perhaps because on the surface it does not seem to be that distinctive. The area around us is relatively young, affluent, well-educated, and about 90 percent white. The dominant congregations are affiliated with well-known denominations: Roman Catholic,

United Methodist, and the Evangelical Lutheran Church of America. However, these villages and towns have their own interesting stories.

We hope that by closing with an exploration of our local religious geography, we will inspire you to go out and explore your own. We also hope to illustrate how some of the themes we encountered throughout our trip—the influence of immigration and ethnicity in shaping places of faith, the power of innovation and creativity in American religion, and the far-reaching influence of faith communities—apply not only to our own home but likely to yours as well.

ETHNICITY: OLD AND NEW

Wherever we went in the United States, we could not escape the strong connection between ethnicity, race, and religion. The same can be said for central Pennsylvania. When you first visit our hometown of State College, the ethnic and racial diversity of the area seems completely a product of Penn State University. And, indeed, much of it is. When you visit the local Chinese and Korean congregations you find an abundance of Penn State parking stickers. The same is true when you visit the local mosque. Although each of these groups has an interesting story, we want to move beyond the university's influence to two other congregations in the county. One, Gatesburg Lutheran Church, was built in the eighteenth century; the other, the Russian Baptist Church, in the late twentieth. Even though we pass by these congregations regularly, we were not aware of the fascinating stories underlying them.

There is not much left of Gatesburg, a small rural village about fifteen miles southwest of State College. The mailboxes for most residents sit on a single spinning wagon wheel at the main crossroads of town. Throughout the 1800s Gatesburg was known for the nearby iron ore mines. Transporting iron ore helped to grow the community. By the late 1800s, however, the mines began to close, and the small town was destined to become even smaller. The post office, school, and handful of stores are all gone. Only the Lutheran church remains.

The name of the town suggests that it was founded by English settlers, with "Gates" being a common English name and "burg" referring to a town. But the presence of a single Lutheran church and the early names on the church cemetery's tombstones suggest otherwise. When we attended the community's bicentennial celebration in the summer of 2009, read their publications, and talked with church members and residents, we heard many stories about the early German settlers and their many descendents that remain in the area.

The story of Gatesburg begins with Henry Getz. A member of the Pennsylvania Militia during the Revolutionary War, he was granted a warrant to lay claim to large tracts of land in central Pennsylvania. He was joined by fellow Germans, for whom the local church served as the center for preserving their heritage. A couple of years after the town was plotted and settlers began arriving in 1808, the first Lutheran church was founded. At first, it was a modest twenty-foot by twenty-foot log cabin, but it grew to twenty by forty during the Civil War. After fires destroyed the first two wooden churches, the congregation decided that brick might be the way to go, and in 1913 they built the church that is still standing today. Although records are fuzzy, it is clear that sermons were given in both German and English at least in the early 1800s, and likely later. German was also used in the local public schools where students were taught the German Psalter (biblical psalms used in worship). For many generations the church remained the center of town life, where each new generation learned what it meant to be a German Lutheran in America.

By the middle of the nineteenth century, however, with tensions rising over recent waves of German and Irish Catholic immigrants, the old German families began to hide their heritage. Getz was changed to the English sounding Gates, the Romelbarge family altered their surname to Rumbarger, the Reubers became Riders, and Herbster was now Harpster. Because children who spoke with a German accent were disparagingly called "little Dutchies" in the early twentieth century, parents started to avoid speaking German to their children. Two hundred years after the founding of the congregation, the Gates, Riders, and Harpsters still live in the area, and several still attend the local Lutheran church. But worshiping in German is a distant memory, and the distinctive German practices have been crowded out by new traditions distinctive to Gatesburg, Pennsylvania.

If ethnicity has faded at the Gatesburg Lutheran Church, however, it is very much alive at the local Russian Baptist

The Russian Baptist Church in State College, Pennsylvania was the product of historical events and chance personal connections coming together to plant a Russian speaking community in the middle of Pennsylvania.

Church just outside of State College. The church was founded only in 1988, but its story is filled with unexpected twists, turns, and ironies. For starters, most of the members aren't Russian. Immigrants from the former Soviet Union, the congregants' common language is Russian, but they are primarily from Kazakhstan and Ukraine. Equally surprising is that the congregation is Baptist rather than one of the dominant religions of their native countries: Orthodox Christian or Muslim. And, perhaps most surprising, they are already one of the largest churches in the State College area, seating approximately seven hundred people in their worship area.

So, why did they end up in State College and how did it happen so fast? The story begins in 1986, when a Baptist preacher named Ruvim had a vision that the Soviet Union would soon fall apart and that believers should leave. Knowing that his parents had Baptist friends who had immigrated to the United States in 1929, Ruvim began writing letters in an effort to locate his friends' daughter. After mailing thirty letters from fifteen different Soviet cities, he eventually found her. Initially, Ruvim, his wife, and three of his married children and their families were given permission to emigrate. After finding their way to State College, and to the daughter of his parents' friends, they began encouraging other family members, including their many in-laws, to immigrate. The result is a "Russian" congregation that now has approximately 350 people attending worship services each week.

The ethnic identity of this congregation remains strong. Russian is spoken at all of the worship services. Yet there are also signs that the younger generation is gradually moving beyond the ethnic enclave of their parents. When our colleague, Catherine Wanner, first began visiting the church in 1998, she reported that "very few of the parents, and almost none of the grandparents, spoke any English." Twelve years later the parents were increasingly fluent in English, and the children relied on classes at church to learn how to read and write Russian. One member commented, "my teenage daughter can read and write Russian well, but I won't be surprised if her children never learn Russian." The linguistic and cultural gap continues to widen between the generations. Like the Danish Lutherans of Dannebrog, Nebraska, or the Lebanese Muslims in Dearborn, Michigan, the second and third generations of the Russian Baptist Church are increasingly embedded in the larger culture and increasingly relying on English.

RELIGIOUS INNOVATIONS

When making his case for religious freedom in the new American nation, Thomas Jefferson assured his critics that freedom allows all religions to "flourish." Our tour found support for his argument. Protected by laws mandating religious freedom, new religions are constantly arising, and existing religions are experimenting with new innovations. The innovations are most glaring in Houston, but we found them everywhere we went. As we looked closer in central Pennsylvania, we found them here, too.

We first learned about Mercy Hill from a student intern named Jennifer McClure. She encouraged us to visit the nontraditional evangelical church meeting in a local movie theater. Before we went, we checked their website, the opening page of which displayed a three-word message: "Relevance Shows Reverence." Below the text was an arm covered with colorful tattoos and holding what appeared to be a Bible. But if the website's appearance was nontraditional, the statement of faith was not. It proclaimed a belief in the inspiration and authority of the Bible, the deity of Jesus Christ, and the redemption of sinful humans through Jesus Christ.

We arrived in time to see a truck and trailer backed up to the College 9 Theatre. Used to transport the church's sound

Demonstrating that a church does not require its own building, the Mercy Hill congregation in State College, Pennsylvania meets in a movie theater.

system, coffee bar, and Sunday school supplies each week, the trailer serves as the weekday home for virtually all of the church's belongings. When you enter the theater-church, you are greeted by an unusual mixture of sights and smells. One banner welcomes you to Mercy Hill, and a nearby poster advertises a movie "now showing." A second banner marking the prayer room is placed next to a video game. The aroma of freshly brewed coffee is mixed with the smell of last night's popcorn. But after you get past the nontraditional setting, this congregation's coffee time was similar to most.

As worship time approached, we heard the band playing in a theater down the hall. Mercy Hill rents three of the theaters, one for worship and two for child instruction and care. When we entered the worship theater, the lights were dim and the screen displayed the words to the songs, with other graphics and artwork in the background. When the music came to a stop, visitors were welcomed and given a free box of popcorn, announcements were made, and then the sermon began. Given that a movie would be shown in the theater at noon, we knew the service could not go much past 11:45 a.m.

When we spoke with the pastor, Keith Davis, after the service, he said that they like to "do church outside of the box." He stressed that the church needs to be relevant and meet people where they are. As we spoke, the sound system, coffee bar, and pop-up banners were all being loaded into the trailer once more. Before the movie fans began to arrive, the portable church was gone . . . until next week.

As we continued to explore our own hometown, we quickly learned that Mercy Hill was neither the only portable church nor the most recent new church. Other portable congregations were meeting in schools and storing their church property in trailers similar to Mercy Hill's, and other new churches were renting spaces from established churches or were still meeting in their congregants' homes. But we also found some groups gathering in people's homes that never planned to move out.

Ken Layng, a member of a local "house" church, as such groups are known, explained that despite their radical departure from a traditional church structure, most house churches strive to support the "core" teachings of Christianity. He explained that their worship services are more flexible than other Christian churches, but they still include singing, praying, and the study of biblical passages. They also celebrate the Christian practice of Holy Communion and conduct baptisms. Ken showed us pictures of a baptism in a local backyard pool. Unlike many other new religious groups meeting in homes, however, the house churches do not aspire to become "full size" churches. Instead, they are expected to split into multiple house churches when they become too large for a single house. Ken noted that the ideal size of a congregation is usually between six and sixteen adults.

Part of a larger "house church movement," the members attempt to step away from the institutional church, eschew hierarchies, and return to what they view as the small Christian gatherings of the early New Testament era. Like so many "new" changes we saw, the movement is justified as an innovative return to an earlier, purer practice of their faith.

REACHING OUT

Congregations are clearly the anchor of American religion. But as we toured communities across the country, we found the influence of congregations consistently extends into the larger neighborhood, community, and culture. Many congregations support the national and international parachurch organizations we visited in Colorado Springs. Congregations in central Pennsylvania are involved in many parachurch

Members of the State College Christian Church unload their "church in a box." The congregation meets in the gymnasium of a school.

efforts as well. For example, the local chapter of Habitat for Humanity relies on congregations to mobilize members and financial contributions for its building projects. Even many of the parachurch groups on Penn State's campus frequently turn to local congregations for support.

But the missions of the local congregations are not limited to assisting parachurch organizations or larger missions. Many congregations take on outreach independently or in cooperation with other local congregations. In cities across America we found single congregations or groups of local congregations

Volunteer workers at the FaithCentre food bank in Bellefonte,
Pennsylvania sort produce donated by local churches. FaithCentre is
a Christian nonprofit that provides a variety of social services. It works
closely with local congregations.

sponsoring food banks, parochial schools, English classes for
immigrants, sports and music programs, social services, and
many other activities that reach beyond the local congregation.

In State College, four of the county's seven food banks
were started by local churches, and most continue to rely on
local churches for volunteers. They also benefit from congregational donations, including produce from a large vegetable
garden jointly farmed by four local churches. The congregations in our community are also active in education and
childcare. An evangelical Protestant church and a Roman
Catholic parish each have elementary schools, and several
other congregations support preschools, daycare centers,
and jointly sponsored high schools. A large youth football

program sponsored by the Assemblies of God church offers another example, and the list goes on and on.

As we spoke with more pastors and church members, however, we soon learned that their outreach goes far beyond the local community. State College Christian Church, a small congregation of about 150 members, offers one of the most prominent examples. They rent the gym of a grade school to use for their Sunday service and store virtually all of the congregation's possessions in a utility trailer during the week. Unlike many congregations using trailers, State College Christian is not a new start-up. Until recently, they owned their own church building just a few blocks from where they now worship. They sold the building and moved to the gym when the congregation decided that the edifice was receiving too much of their attention while too little of their time and resources were being given to missions.

Shortly after their move to the school gym, the congregation began mission work in Zambia. At first, they donated to a large international parachurch group, World Vision, to purchase blankets for children. During a mission trip in 2005, however, Pastor Smith met the Zambian native John Banda, who encouraged him to provide support for orphans at a school Banda runs. Initially, the children of the church raised $800, enough to support three orphans. Then, Mr. Banda asked if they could support fifteen more orphans. Support for those additional fifteen were followed by fifteen more, until the congregation was sponsoring forty-six children. Given the high level of support, Banda renamed the school: State College Christian Church School for the

Orphans in Zambia. Ninety percent of the families in the small church are now sponsoring a child in Zambia. Many of the sponsors have met the children because the congregation organizes an annual mission trip to Zambia. By 2010 State College Christian Church was partnering with five other small congregations to support eighty-six children and two schools in Zambia, now named Haven of Hope.

The story of State College Christian Church is no doubt exceptional for the area. At least that's what we had assumed. But as we talked with other pastors and toured their churches, we learned that many congregations took international mission trips and formed partnerships with congregations in other countries. For other congregations the outreach was local or included less "hands-on" activities. But virtually all of the churches had an outreach that extended beyond their own group.

ENDING OUR JOURNEY

We hope that this chapter has shown you that you do not need to embark on a six-week road trip to appreciate the unique aspects of America's religious geography. We began this book by describing *Places of Faith* as a journey—a journey across the country to discover America's unique religious landscape. We confess that our journey is far from over. For each new discovery, we uncovered a plethora of new questions. For each new experience, we found so many more to explore. We hope that some of the information has been useful, exciting, and even fun. But our greatest hope is that it will spur others to explore the ever changing religious geography of America.

REFERENCES AND FURTHER READING

Harpster, Ernie et al. 2009. *Glimpses of Gatesburg and Surrounding Areas, 1809–2009.* Gatesburg Historical Committee.

Haven of Hope. 2010. http://www.havenofhopezambia.org/, accessed on August 24, 2010.

Viola, Frank. 2010. Present Testimony Ministry http://www.ptmin.org/, accessed on August 24, 2010.

Wanner, Catherine. 2007. *Communities of the Converted: Ukrainians and Global Evangelism.* Ithaca, NY: Cornell University Press.

INDEX